What People Are Saying About
The Art of the Nudge:

"A fresh and innovative look at how the brain works and how you can inspire others through effective storytelling and a variety of techniques. *The Art of the Nudge* is pertinent to all in business. This exciting work is also appropriate for anyone who needs to motivate recalcitrant family members."

— Chris Rice, President and CEO of Blessing-White, Author of *The Engagement Equation*

"As a fellowship trained Board Certified Orthopaedic Surgeon specializing in spinal disorders, I have read *The Art of the Nudge* with great interest. Having done both basic science and clinical research in biopsychosocial and behavioral topics, I believe John and Christine have taken their combined skill sets and created a programmed series of steps to tap effectively the unlimited potential of the human brain and impact behavioral economics favorably. One of the many joys of reading their book was the style and readability utilized when addressing some very complex and potentially transformative subjects. Every leader interested in learning how to achieve more with effective utilization of energy, time, and resources will benefit from learning the stories contained within this book."

— Ron Wisneski, M.D., Medical Director of Beebe HealthyBack

D0008806

"For personal, professional, and leadership development, *The Art of the Nudge* is now at the top of my recommended reading list! John Geraci and Christine Miles have developed a strategic communication framework, based on scientific brain research and observations, to help us determine what we want to do and why, and to learn how to use the Story Engine, personality profiles, and Nudges to inspire success. A great book full of strategies for leadership teams to read, discuss, and use for positive results."

— Dr. Pat Long, President Emeritus of Baker University, with 30 years experience in Higher Education

"If you have ever thought you might have untapped potential, this book will both prove it to you as well as introduce a communication framework to help unleash it. As a Yoga Studio owner and Health Coach, I teach the power of connection through small, mindful actions. *The Art of the Nudge* simplifies how we achieve personal and professional growth. It relays impactful and motivating principles, such as slowing down to speed up, and shows us anything can be learned, practiced, and mastered. This book inspired me to think somewhat differently, and I will be sharing it with my students and communities."

— Eve D'Onofrio, Founder of Health Tribes
& Priya Hot Yoga

"*The Art of the Nudge* is a mind-opening 'must read' book. Christine Miles and John Geraci have melded their knowledge and experience to create a strong potion combining psychology, communication, and process to 'nudge' people and organizations to deliver successful business outcomes. The power of story, in particular Story Gathering, has done more for tearing down walls, building teamwork, and building closer relations internally and externally than anything I have ever experienced in my career."

— Frank Rhea, Executive VP, Tozour Energy Systems

"By implementing the synthesizing strategies and techniques described in this book, my technology services company was able to complete a performance and cultural transformation that has seen it grow annual revenues fivefold, annual backlog sevenfold, and triple its balance sheet during my tenure. Because it reflects basic human nature, CI Squared's framework has been easy and very natural for our service- and technology-oriented employees to adopt and maintain in operation, unlike more process and stage gate-oriented practices. I strongly recommend that you utilize the methods and underlying logic described here."

— Bill Mahoney, CEO, South Carolina
Research Authority, Columbia, SC

"As a trained lawyer, former CEO of the Kansas City Foundation, and active software entrepreneur, I was an early adopter of TATN and reader of *The Art of the Nudge*. I have been actively using this communication framework to help me 'slow down' and better Gather other people's stories first, before telling my own stories to create Nudges. Clarifying the 'WHYs' for my business and becoming a much better practitioner of Story Gathering has helped me immensely in communicating with my senior leadership team and customers. I am recommending this book to all of my CEO colleagues because I strongly believe in both the complex ideas presented and the simple and effective framework to build these skills. Everyone who interacts with people can benefit from *The Art of the Nudge*."

— Laura Wells McKnight, Executive, Attorney, and Author

A LEADERSHIP COMMUNICATION FRAMEWORK TO
INSPIRE YOU AND YOUR ORGANIZATION TO TAKE ACTION

THE ART  OF THE

UNLOCKING
YOUR HIDDEN
POTENTIAL

JOHN GERACI
CHRISTINE MILES

AVIVA
PUBLISHING
New York

THE ART OF THE Nudge
UNLOCKING YOUR HIDDEN POTENTIAL

Published by:
Aviva Publishing
Lake Placid, NY
(518) 523-1320
www.AvivaPubs.com

CI Squared LLC
Telephone: (609) 516-9833
Email: jgeraci@cisquared.net
       cmiles@cisquared.net
http://cisquared.net

ISBN: 9781943164134
Library of Congress: 2015907642

Editors: Tyler Tichelaar and Sarah Dickinson
Cover Designer: Nicole Gabriel /Angel Dog Productions
Interior Book Layout: Nicole Gabriel /Angel Dog Productions
Illustrators: Alexis Garapola, Jennifer Dickinson, and Sarah Dickinson

Every attempt has been made to source properly all quotes.

Printed in the United States of America
First Edition

Contents

Acknowledgments:

John Geraci

I want to thank my father, Colonel John P. Geraci, for helping me develop a passion for reading and continuous learning. Lucia Geraci, my wife of over forty years, was behind the scenes supporting me and is both my rock and a very wise woman, blessed with good common sense. I want to thank all of my mentors and colleagues who helped me learn, grow, and develop these ideas at West Point, in the military, and in business—many from Management Science America and Advent Software.

I give special thanks to the customers who have lived this journey with Christine and me, especially those who allowed us to tell their stories: SCRA, Compliance Science, Tozour Energy Systems, and Germantown Academy. Several colleagues have played a big role by reading early drafts and providing advice and feedback including Bill Mahoney, Brad Childress, Torbjorn Tenmann, Rich Dillon, Deirdre Sanborn, Frank Libby, and my wife, Lucia. Their insights proved very valuable.

Laura Wells McKnight was instrumental in facilitating the editing process and guiding us along the way. Sarah Dickinson, our trusted colleague at CI^2, was tireless in her efforts to research, edit, and get the details correct, while Alexis Garapola used her art talents and passion to turn our picture ideas into something useable and fun.

My biggest acknowledgment goes to my business partner, Christine Miles. Her brainpower, point-of-view, and ability to disagree agreeably while leading us to other creative ideas and solutions was monumental. This book has been a true integration of our ideas, both from our individual experiences over the years and our collaboration in studying, testing, and applying our knowledge to real customer situations; we have constantly improved and adapted throughout this process. The journey has been long, with some struggles along the way, but extremely rewarding. We hope we have created something meaningful.

Christine Miles

I want to thank my mother, Susan, for teaching me to have a genuine curiosity and interest in people. I would like to thank my father, Charles, for being the best example of what it means to have a strong work ethic. In addition to what he taught me about business, he instilled in me the idea that I had no limitations based on my gender.

I want to thank three of my coaches/mentors: Linda Kreiser, Carol Miller, and Andy Fussner. They each saw my untapped potential, rather than my more obvious limitations. Collectively, they helped me achieve greater success both athletically and professionally than I could have ever dreamed to achieve without them. I also thank my ex-husband and lifelong friend, Michael, for supporting me throughout the years and always wanting more for me than I could want for myself.

I give special thanks to my clients and friends, Frank Rhea and Sue Szczepkowski, for being wonderful examples of great leadership and for being vulnerable and making others want to follow them. I have watched and learned from them over the years, and I am better for being in their presence.

Thanks to our colleagues Sarah Dickinson, Laura McKnight, and Jennifer Dickinson for their tireless efforts and collaboration in the development of the book; their individual talents and collective contributions have been invaluable.

More than anyone, I would like to thank my business partner, John, for his generosity, his tenacity, and his strategic and brilliant mind. He is a mentor who has made a difference in the lives of so many over the course of his forty-year career, and I thank him for making a difference in my life every day.

And finally, thanks to Jess for bringing love and light into my life in a way I never thought was possible.

Introduction

This book came about almost by chance; it was serendipitous. Christine and I did not meet one another until 2011. It was at a seminar on storytelling, and for some reason, we just hit it off. We come from very different professional backgrounds. Christine is an Ivy League graduate of the University of Pennsylvania and an accomplished athlete. She spent her professional career in psychological services, migrating to Leadership/Management Training and Executive Coaching, helping organizations and several Fortune 500 CEOs develop their talents and produce better results. I am a West Point graduate and Airborne Ranger who, upon finishing with the military, entered into an executive career in the software industry, leading high-growth companies.

Despite our differences, Christine and I realized pretty quickly that we shared a lot of similar beliefs about people and organizations and that our different perspectives are actually very complementary. We both believe that people and organizations have tremendous untapped potential to grow and change. We both acknowledge that people will resist change because it's hard. For example, we have all seen athletes who could have achieved more in their sports and organizations that have stagnated because of their inabilities to innovate. We have also seen wildly successful companies struggle to adapt to new environments, and as a result, begin to atrophy and die.

The thing we were most interested in though is: Why? If people really do have more potential, what is the source of it? Is there a more powerful way to unleash it to help people act more decisively and achieve more in these fast-paced times? We felt that if we combined the different angles from which we approached this question, it would offer a wider lens to observe and understand it.

Of course, any discussion about the topic also had to acknowledge the macro trends and their impact on organizations and the people that work in them; e.g.:

- The faster pace and amount of technological change: the combination of social/digital/mobile delivered in the cloud has led to the explosive growth of data and data analytics (Big Data). And the Internet of things (IOT) is still in its embryonic stage. We believe this trend is only going to accelerate.

- Millennials now make up the largest population cohort/group. This generation born roughly between the early 1980s and early 2000s is a larger population than baby boomers and is becoming a major force in the economy as both consumers and workers. This group's values, needs, wants, and ways of working are different and will cause the same kinds of disruptions and opportunities that the baby boomers who preceded them did.

We think the effects of these macro trends on all of us are:

- The world seems to be moving faster: Twenty-four hours in a day is no longer enough time to accomplish everything we set out to do.

- Shorter attention spans: Everyone seems to have less time and is always pressing on to the next thing. We are bombarded by constant inputs from email, Facebook, Twitter, LinkedIn, Instagram, Snap Chat, or any of the other tools available to help us communicate and collaborate. Despite having all this new technology to link us, in many ways, people and organizations have never felt more disconnected.

- Shifting priorities: What's important at any given moment can change a lot more quickly than in the past. And despite the number of new communication vehicles at our disposal, we tend to be less aware than ever about others' shifting priorities—in both personal and business situations. This lack of other-awareness results in confusion, poor alignment, and just plain miscommunication.

These trends have all been written about before, but Christine and I do not believe organizations truly understand their current and future impacts. They demand different solutions for products, processes, culture, and leadership for nearly every organization. And they require people and organizations to learn and adapt more quickly and continuously than ever before.

We wanted to understand better the negative effects of these trends. Does this greater dependence on technology and this faster pace of change help or hinder our ability to act and grow? Could there be a better way? We felt that if people and organizations could pivot more quickly, and act more decisively in the face of struggles, they might achieve more. This book is our story of how we went about confirming our beliefs and creating a communication framework to unleash more of people's potential to act, grow, and achieve.

Christine and I spent three years working together on field research with organizations and studying the latest research on brain science, behavioral economics, communication theory, and the concept of story and leadership. Interacting with our clients, both large and small organizations, in everyday business situations while studying the latest theories and ideas brought real world clarity and needs into our aperture, sparking some innovative concepts.

We found startling new developments and insights have resulted from research done by neuroscientists about both the capacity and workings of the human brain (Kaku, *The Future of the Mind*). These new concepts showed that we not only have untapped potential but almost unlimited potential, and if we could harness the brain's capacity even a little more than we were currently doing, it would have a big effect on results and performance. We thought that this research was profound, and it inspired us to see whether we could come up with a way to make it practical.

Our differing perspectives led to some constructive conflict and creative tension. Through persistence, curiosity, and pure gumption, we experienced what we felt was a significant breakthrough. If you believe, as we do, that the brain has tremendous unused power and potential, then maybe the Mind vs. Matter and Nature vs. Nurture discussions, which have been debated throughout history as far back as Aristotle, were inaccurate. What if potential could be tapped into with an AND, not an OR—harnessing the power of both? What if we "slowed down to speed up" and shifted and grew with small "Nudges" vs. pushing people to make large changes? These seemed like game-changing ideas to us, but we felt we had to test them out in real life with real companies to see whether they worked and added value.

Christine and I began to codify what we were learning into a framework that helped us shift our dialogue of Mind vs. Matter and Nature vs. Nurture to a new model—one that integrates these historically juxtaposed ideas into a more powerful lever, turning vs./or into an

AND. We call our communication framework, The Art of the Nudge (TATN)™. It's based on two core principles: "Slow down to speed up," and "Small Nudges can inspire action." We believe strongly that these principles empower us to harness our potential more fully in these fast-paced times, helping to break through all of the noise and clutter. We hope that you will use the TATN Framework to unleash more of your untapped potential and to take Action on things you want to accomplish for yourself and/or your organization.

Maybe at this point you are thinking: *So what? Why should I care about this?* Well, Christine and I think that most individuals are looking for continuous ways to improve and innovate. Do you, as a leader, believe you have already maximized your own or your organization's potential? If you take the time to "slow down" a little and learn more about the power of your brain and how it works, we are convinced you can apply this knowledge in some way you are not envisioning now. Understanding the current breakthroughs in neuroscience and their implications is really necessary to knowing how to unleash more of this potential for better organizational results such as revenue growth, greater profitability, and increased customer satisfaction and employee engagement, all leading to increasing shareholder value.

We believe that current neuroscience shows our brains to be more quantum than mechanical and that understanding how our brains and personalities drive actions and habits can help us unlock more of our potential.

Additionally, this understanding will debunk some of the prevailing and inhibiting ideas that have been traditionally taught. How many times have you said or heard things like, "People are just who they are and cannot change," or "You can't teach an old dog new tricks," or "I do it this way because I always have"?

This book will introduce you to a new way of thinking through visual concepts such as: "The Iceberg," "The Elephant and Rider," and "Superhighways and Dirt Roads." These metaphors will help you understand your massive potential, and help unlock and integrate the power of your conscious and subconscious brains.

Christine and I also share some startling breakthroughs designed to help you understand how we and others take Action, and what keeps us doing some things habitually while avoiding other things. Then we will describe "The Art of the Nudge™," our five-step communication framework to inspire people to Action, as well as some other powerful tools that complement the steps of TATN. These tools support finding and taking "small nudges" that deliver significant results.

This book also shares some stories with you to illustrate the application of these concepts in real-life situations: The story of South Carolina Research Authority (SCRA) and its Nudge for the business development team that helped it grow from $100 million to over $400 million in revenue, while growing its backlog to over $1 billion; Compliance Science, which applied our CCSA process to ignite its sales team to higher performance; and our own story of slowing down and using personality profiles to help us win new clients and increase our own revenue stream.

Personality Profiles, Story, and Nudges are complementary TATN tools, and we provide detailed examples of how and when to use them. We also illustrate the reasons why our personalities are formed very early, maybe in the womb, and how we can FLEX in order to adapt to be more effective with ourselves and others. You will see that although we all judge personalities, we are often mistaken, and there are powerful tools to be found in uncovering core personalities that will assist in understanding both ourselves and others, while helping us flex our own style.

We also tell you about the power of "Story"—both Gathering and Telling, the importance of each and when to do each, and what types of stories you need to have in your arsenal to Nudge yourself and others to Action. You will also learn about Story Gathering and why most people do not do it well. We have seen that when you become a skillful practitioner with this tool of Story Gathering, you will differentiate yourself exponentially and align with others like never before. We discuss the art of nudging others, and how to stay patient enough to get someone's full story. You will see that "slowing down to speed up" is a very powerful concept that can be learned, practiced, and mastered.

This book will take you through each step of TATN in detail, as well as show you how applying the related tools can get you to effective Nudges quickly. Once you learn this Nudge or the "how" of the tool, you will only be constrained by your willingness to use it, and it will be easy to tell the right stories. Of course, some people will do it more naturally, but we conclude the book with a chapter showing how all of us can learn and practice these tools until they become second nature. We call it The Art of the Nudge (TATN)™ because it is very easy to do if you decide to, and when done correctly, you can create small Nudges and Action for substantive results. We have not created a complicated program here. We are not asking you or others to take huge leaps that you will not take. Rather, we are nudging you in a way to make action simple and doable while yielding tremendous results.

Christine and I have done extensive readings on current theory and thinking for this book on the following topics:

1. The Brain/Neuroscience and how it really works
2. Behavioral Economics and how people make buying decisions
3. Psychological Studies on communication and what the best communicators do that most of us don't
4. A Study of Leaders and what makes them effective

We have synthesized this information and combined it

with our own "real world" personal struggles and those of our clients. Because our brains have almost unlimited capacity and ability to absorb and process information, we know that we have hit upon an incredible idea—a Nudge so simple and effective that we have been personally using it and testing it with our clients over the last few years. We believe that TATN will help you inspire people to action, unleashing more of the potential in your organization, and we hope that we have created enough curiosity for you to take a leap of faith to read this book and try it.

Along the way, Christine and I merged our businesses, renaming our joined company "CI Squared LLC" or just CI². It stands for Continuous Improvement and Innovation, which is what our communication framework will empower you to accomplish in business and in life. We hope you will enjoy this book and get a tremendous reward through our Nudge, and that our humanness and vulnerability will come through as we share Our Story.

John Christine

Chapter 1:

A New Way of Thinking—The Art of the Nudge™ (TATN)

How Our Story Begins

Christine and I met at a seminar on storytelling three years ago. We were both intrigued by the idea that such an ancient art was both a potentially powerful tool, and that it had mostly been forgotten by our rushed and harried digital society. During the workshop, we did a few exercises telling and listening to stories. It became apparent that we were much clearer, crisper, and more memorable when we were telling stories rather than reading bulleted PowerPoint slides. Both of us came from the corporate world where PowerPoint with 10-12 bullet points per slide was the norm. We knew that when others read their presentations verbatim to us from slides, we nodded off. Of course, it never dawned on us that we were sleeping machines as well. Go figure.

For some reason, Christine and I just hit it off. Among many other things, I found out that she had been a highly accomplished field hockey player, and it so happened that I had just completed a five-year journey of coaching a high school girls lacrosse team. Maybe it was the competitive spirit, the drive for excellence, or just plain curiosity that caused us to connect, but we did, and we listened to each other's stories. We found out that both of us believed in people's untapped potential for growth and achievement, and that in order to unleash this potential, we all must change. We also know that change is hard both for companies and individuals. We learned that each of us had a passion to help others achieve and perform, and enough curiosity to pursue those ideas together. Although we maintained our independent consulting practices initially, we decided to work together when we could to help companies improve and explore this idea of unleashing potential in a fast-paced world.

Through our shared work experiences, we learned different ideas from one another and our customers. We found that although we shared beliefs and passions, we have different personalities and styles that initially created conflict for us, leading to a tipping point in our partnership. While what we did was similar, the "how" was often different, and through our intensive study on neuroscience and the brain, coupled with real-world practice, we came to an interesting discovery....

The tipping point came as the result of a very good but tense day. Christine and I had been out on meetings and were in the middle of debriefing during the car ride back. I was rushing toward next steps and how to move these people along faster. Christine was not there yet, and we both got pretty frustrated and a little angry with each other. Then she said, "John, slow down." I kind of looked at her in disbelief and she repeated, "Slow down, please." Yes, I am a Type A personality, so when she repeated this again, saying, "Please slow down and let me understand your story. We might get there faster," I was kind of stunned. Since I didn't really know what to say, I just blurted out, "What do you mean?" And Christine said to me, "Take me back in this story and give me more details before we jump to next steps." Well, to be truthful with you, we did not do it that day. Instead, we took a break. What Christine said haunted me all night. Neurons were wiring and firing, and a lot of stuff was brewing under the surface of my mind. We realized we were onto something potentially big, and if we could just meld our styles and strengths while staying curious, this could be a good journey.

Over the next few days, we processed what happened and came to two simple yet impactful ideas: 1) taking the time to get the whole story and understand the story the same way may lead to better alignment and synergy, actually getting us there faster with more creativity, and 2) slowing down to take small nudges allows us to speed up, accelerating performance and inspiring people to take Action. Together, over the last few years, Christine and I have taught workshops to clients, coached executives, and studied topics that we thought might give us some answers: brain science, behavioral economics, communication theory, story, and leadership. The combination of this consulting work and research led us to invent a Communication Framework called "The Art of the Nudge™" (TATN). With this framework, we have helped individuals and companies make small improvements that deliver big results.

We firmly believe that you, as an innovative and curious-minded leader, will benefit by taking the time to understand this revolution in brain science and its implications. This understanding is necessary to knowing how to unleash more potential for better organizational results: revenue growth, greater profitability, increased customer satisfaction and employee engagement, all leading to increased shareholder value. However, let's not get too far ahead of ourselves.

Why Are We Humans Who We Are and What Potential Do We Really Have?

While attending the Infantry Officer Advance Course in 1978, I heard a professor from the University of Colorado give a speech titled, "What You Are Now Is Where You Were When." He postulated that most of us had completed our major development around age six, and that our norms, values, and major perceptions were pretty much locked in. His view was that people would not fundamentally change unless faced with a significant emotional event that destabilized their thinking and caused a shift.

The professor relayed a story to make his case. It all started with some students at the University of Colorado riding bicycles to class. They began bringing their bikes into the buildings and parking them outside the classrooms. What started out as "cute" when done by two, three, or four students, quickly grew into a nuisance as the movement started trending. It created a large bottleneck and dangerous hazard when everyone was in the corridor trying to avoid bicycles. One day, the professor just plain got fed up. He grabbed a bicycle from one of the students and kicked the spokes in, yelling wildly, "This is what I will do to every bicycle I see back in our buildings!" As you can imagine, the students were both stunned and shocked. How could this mild-mannered psychology professor go off the deep end, start yelling like a madman, and ruin someone's bike? The event triggered a lot of buzz as conversations spread like wildfire throughout the campus. Everyone had an opinion, but they all agreed on one thing: The professor was not kidding. The madman would most likely do it again. And none of them wanted to call his parents and tell them of the crazy professor who ruined his bike. The professor's actions in kicking in the spokes definitely created a significant emotional event for the students.

Not surprisingly, no bikes were to be found in any of the buildings the day after the professor's outburst. The administration was astonished, and quite honestly, the professor was happy, though a little embarrassed. He took this incident to confirm his theory that systems or behaviors in practice could not be changed without people undergoing a significant emotional event.

But Who Are We Really?

The studies of psychology and neuroscience have progressed tremendously in the forty years since the bike incident on the University of Colorado's campus. We know a lot more today about what is going on in the brain. However, step back and imagine our ancestors in the Serengeti. Trying to live, trying to eat, and trying not to be eaten. They walked miles in the desert, hunting other animals. They moved in packs for safety and security. They killed animals and found a way to cook and eat them. They fended off attacks from larger predators. How did they survive in this tough jungle?

Well, as humans, we are amazing creatures. Our brains have been evolving for over 200 million years into the most complex, quantum, and powerful tool known to man. We are all born with 100 billion neurons in our brains. Each neuron contains an axon at the end that can fire neurotransmitters, or electrical and chemical signals, to form a connection with other neurons. This doesn't seem that amazing until you stop to think that each neuron can make 10-15 thousand connections. That is somewhere between 100 trillion and 1,000 trillion connections. Now, when Christine and I first saw these statistics, we could not even comprehend those figures, let alone understand their implications. After verifying that a plethora of brain research confirms these statistics, we accepted this premise.

We later discovered that what actually happens is that we are all born with these 100 billion neurons, and between our birth and age six, those neurons wire and fire, with some actually firing during pre-birth (nature). Based upon our environments, stimuli, care by others, and repetition, we all form connections, some the same, but many different. These connections are what make us unique and help shape our view of the world. When we reach about age six, however, the firings stop occurring, weaning out some of the weaker connections (so as it turns out, the professor from Colorado was onto something). This mental stimulation was fun and positive for growth, but we would be going crazy if our brains kept up that level of activity. In fact, Autistic, Tourette's, and Attention Deficit Disorder (ADD) patients have some of this super-stimulation going on, which impedes their ability to focus.

However, around the time we reach puberty, these neurons start firing again and all of us go through another growth spurt of learning and doing, trying and finding things we like. Think back to what was happening to you when you were fourteen. Likely, that was a high-growth period that strengthened some of your neuron connections and built new ones, and yes, even replaced some old ones. Thus, this complex network of connection is one of the mysteries and capabilities that both makes us human and makes us different. In this book we describe the strong neural connections our brains build as "Superhighways."

Figure 1.1

They are paved, well-known, and easy to travel on. We refer to areas where we have not built strong networks as "Dirt Roads."

They have potholes, are in disrepair, and not so easy to use. However, we can learn how to leverage both as we understand our brains more fully.

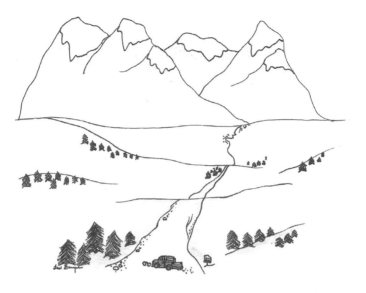

Figure 1.2

Okay, so we've discussed the brain based on its neural connections, but let's go a little deeper. You can think of the brain as being layered and as containing two halves. The layered brain is commonly called the "triune brain" (Kaku 19) and the two halves of the brain are often referred to as the "split left and right brain" (Dr. Roger Sperry, qtd. in Kaku 37). (At this point you may be thinking, "Interesting, but so what?" Well, understanding the way the brain works is important to understanding human behavior and motivation, which is crucial if you want to maximize potential. So hang with us here.) The triune brain evolved over time. The first layer of the brain to develop is called our rep-

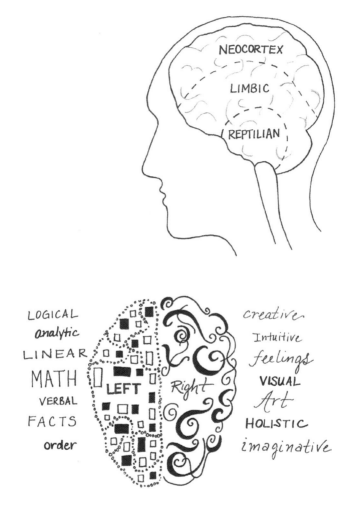

Figure 1.3

tilian brain, and it handles all of our automatic functions, such as breathing and blood flow. Next came our limbic brain, containing two important elements: the hypothalamus and amygdala, which is an extremely powerful part of the brain. The limbic brain evolved over 200 hundred million years ago, and it not only works to create our basic drives, but also our emotions. In discussing the limbic brain, Daniel Siegel, in his book *Mindsight*, states, "It is crucial for how we form relationships and become emotionally attached to one another" (17). This part of the brain triggers all of our emotions, stores all of our autobiographical data, and contains nearly 80 billion neurons. The reptilian and limbic layers of our brains were critical in helping us develop our "Fight or Flight" mechanism for not only thriving, but also surviving. "Evolution designed the human brain not to accurately understand itself but to help us survive" (Mlodinow, *Subliminal* 194).

The third layer of the triune brain is called the neocortex, and it is the least developed part of our brain because it has been evolving for less time. The neocortex is what makes us different and unique to all other animals, and it is where we think, reason, plan, and form language. This part of the brain is like new software version 1.0 compared to our automatic processes that "have been through thousands of product cycles and are nearly perfect" (Haidt 15). The neocortex can only process a few things at a time and works in a more linear fashion. It is deliberate and relatively slow compared to our limbic brain as Daniel Kahneman so aptly describes in *Thinking, Fast and Slow*. These three layers are all connected and work together, but as you will see, sometimes not so easily.

The second way you can think about the brain is it being partitioned into halves, or hemispheres, called the left brain and the right brain (See Figure 1.3 on page 34). The left brain is more logical, analytical, and deals with language. The right brain is more expressive, creative, and innovative. We often think of ourselves as strictly right brain creative or left brain analytical, but in reality, we are all utilizing both hemispheres of the brain, with one hemisphere just being more dominant than the other. These two hemispheres are connected and, therefore, communicate through a bundle of neural fibers called the corpus callosum. As Christine will remind me frequently, neuroscientists know that women have something akin to the fastest data connection known to man (T-3 line) and men mostly have dial-up connections, think AOL circa 1996. It explains why the book *Men are from Mars, Women are from Venus* by John Gray may be accurate, and why women can generally multitask and process emotions better than men due to this faster communication between the left and right brain hemispheres.

With all this said, the brain sounds like a complex tool, but how does it work? Since Ancient Greece, both philosophers and scientists have been searching for the answer about mind over matter. They knew we had a logical, reasoning brain that we could use to think, analyze, and develop language in order to express our ideas. They also realized that we have an emotional, instantaneous brain that leads us to do things we really do not want to do, react immediately to situations, and develop perceptions that turn out to be wrong. This Mind vs. Matter question has been grappled with over the years by Aristotle, Descartes, and Einstein, among others. The debate has raged, and certainly each one of us knows it well in relation to things we do not like to do but do anyway, such as smoking, drinking too much, overeating, and blurting out something when we do not mean to. Think of something you do that you wish you could stop. How easy or hard is it?

Today, we know more about the brain than at any other time, including that the triune brain works together and the left/right brain also work together. Current neuroscientists and behavioral economists call this our "conscious brain" and our "subconscious brain." Mdlodinow states in *Subliminal* that "the current revolution in thinking about the [subconscious] came about because, with modern instruments, [namely, fMRI technology], we can watch as different structures and substructures in the brain generate feelings and emotions" (15). We liken this concept to a large iceberg. Our conscious brain, neocortex, or "mind" is the tip of the iceberg, and the subconscious brain and limbic center is the submerged part.

Figure 1.4

Yes, information comes from below, and we can synthesize it, organize it, plan for it, and discuss it, but the subconscious brain also continues to work on its own. When it interacts with anything—person or situation—it makes a very fast association with the data stored in our 100 trillion connections. As a result, we know immediately whether we like, dislike, know, or don't know something. The subconscious brain is automatic and can often be very good, especially for fight-or-flight decisions such as, "I will not touch that red hot stove again." However, it can also be bad because the correlation or perception it generates may not be accurate, but it's what we have in the connection; for example, "I don't like Bill because he reminds me of a guy in high school whom I disliked." Interesting, but do you really know Bill at all?

Jonathan Haidt in *The Happiness Hypothesis* says, "The metaphor of the rider on an elephant fits [brain] findings more closely. Reason and emotion must both work together" (13).

Figure 1.5

However, if the limbic or subconscious brain is a large, powerful elephant that can go where it wants, how do we guide it? The rider can certainly control the elephant when it is docile or doing something benign, but what about when it is overdrinking or talking too much or yelling angrily at someone either in a business or personal situation?

Figure 1.6

How do we tame this emotional elephant on a focused mission? How can the rider exert more control? Ray Dalio, founder of the investment firm Bridgewater Associates, makes this critical point: "Don't let your emotions hijack your thinking" (qtd. in Hess 31). Therefore, how can we get our thoughts and emotions to work more closely together to achieve what we want to achieve; do what we think we want to do; and stop doing things that we consciously say we do not want to do? So Christine and I asked ourselves, "If this is true about the power of our brain, how could we learn to harness it to take action and grow?"

Why Is Change Hard?

We now know that we all are very complex people. We have a powerful quantum tool in our heads, the brain. Niels Bohr, the Danish Physicist stated, "Anyone who is not shocked by quantum theory has not understood it" (qtd. in Schwartz and Begley 83). The brain has made trillions of connections over the years based upon our specific experiences, relationships, cultures, norms, values, and repetitions. Only part of the brain makes up our conscious mind, or "rider," and is controlled relatively easily. The larger part of our brain lies in the subconscious realm, known as the "elephant," and is more stubborn, automatic, and not so easily tamed.

Additionally, in order to take a new action, we have to take a dirt road and divert from the more powerful superhighways we already know. However, even when we *know* we should take a different road, our elephant is familiar with the superhighways and may not want to take the unknown or unproven path. Anthropologists have studied peoples and cultures for years and determined that it is really hard to make changes. How many of us go on diets initially, stop smoking (not quit), make a vow to change something we don't like, and then, give up? Well, the truth is that change is hard for two reasons. At the subconscious or elephant level, we are already *programmed* to do the thing we are doing, and it becomes automatic. We have a lot of connections, experiences, and repetitions that make it simple and easy to do. Secondly, we are *afraid* of new things. Our conscious brain, or rider, puts up blockages, reasons out what could go wrong, and just plain feels uncomfortable taking that new dirt road.

Christine shared something with me on the way to a workshop one day that boldly makes this point. Here is her story in her words:

> When I was thirty-one years old, I was in the hospital yet again from issues related to a cervical spine injury I suffered in a car accident. I remember this particular day like it was yesterday. At the time, I had been dealing with daily debilitating pain and was on a relentless quest for almost two years to find a treatment that would restore my life to normalcy. It was ten o'clock at night and visiting hours were over at the hospital. I was feeling alone and very agi-

tated from my neck pain. The antibiotics were not helping, and I was just sick of sitting in my room. I decided to walk the halls in the hopes that I could settle myself down.

As I was pushing my cumbersome I.V. cart in my lovely hospital gown, I turned the corner of the hallway and saw a woman wearing a bandana on her head who was also pushing an I.V. cart. As we came face to face, we both looked at each other and realized that we knew one another. Neither one of us was immediately recognizable to the other in our current state or context, but it soon dawned on me that this woman was a former client of mine, Mika, whom I had counseled through a family tragedy several years earlier. We had developed a deep connection and bond. Upon mutually recognizing one another, we were delighted to see each other again, although we were in disbelief that we should meet under these circumstances. This realization first led to some hearty laughter and then to some very heavy conversation. I guessed from the bandana on her head that Mika had lost her hair to cancer treatment.

Mika, thirty-seven years old at the time, went on to describe her story and struggle with rectal cancer, highlighting that the odds of surviving were not in her favor. I could see she was fighting the disease bravely. She then asked me to relate my story, so I told her about the past two years and my struggles after the car accident. What Mika said next truly shocked and astonished me, "Wow, I am so glad I don't have what you have!" After catching my breath, I asked in disbelief, "But, how can that be? Yes, what I have absolutely sucks, and is life-altering, but what you have is life threatening and you could die." Mika, with contentment on her face, said, "Yes, but I know what I am dealing with. I know what I have to do. I would have no idea how to deal with your injury, and I am even afraid to think of tackling it."

Now from a logical, rational perspective, this does not make sense. Would you rather struggle with a tough injury from which you could definitely recover, or face late-stage cancer that could kill you? We have no doubt what most of you would answer while calmly reading this book, but what if you were living it? Mika had adapted to her situation. It was tremendously tough, but it became a highway she knew, and from that she drew comfort. She had learned how her rider could control the elephant, and she was hopeful that she would survive. Mika had no idea of Christine's dirt road. She did not want to start down that new path of the unknown. Change is hard and there is fear in what we do not know.

Consider, for a moment, passengers on a sinking ship. When a ship is going down, when do most of the passengers leave their staterooms? You may guess that the answer is immediately because that thought process is rational and logical. However, you may be surprised to know that leaving immediately is not what most people do. Yes, some early adopters go first, but the bulk of the people finally leave when they discover water in their staterooms over their ankles. "Holy mackerel!" you say? "How can that be?" The rider may have an early indication that you should leave, but you are going to have to pull the elephant kicking and screaming the whole way. I mean, you have been in your lovely stateroom enjoying the air conditioning, big screen TV, and beautiful balcony view of the ocean. It is nice, warm, safe, and cozy. Suddenly, you are informed that the ship is going down and you have to leave this place to go out there and jump in some rickety lifeboat, without food or water and with fifty other people you don't know, most of whom are likely cannibals. At that point, you may be thinking, "The voice coming over the PA system can't be correct! We can't be sinking. I mean I don't even see any water." So you stay put.

Now, consider what happens when water gets over the elephant's ankles; different neurons fire and a new connection is made. The elephant says, "I have seen this *Titanic* movie before. The water starts here, rushes into the hallways and I can't get anywhere." Suddenly, you are envisioning a different story than the cozy stateroom: You see the water rising rapidly. You start rushing around wildly to find air pockets, holding your breath with lungs burning. It becomes really hard to move in those small corridors, and you cannot see very well with all of the water swirling around. You now realize that staying in your room is not going to end well and that you could die in some stupid ship upside down in the ocean. Sadly, you remember that you even missed the scene with Kate Winslet on the mast. What a tragedy. This new story urges your elephant and rider to take action. Get out of that seemingly warm, safe stateroom while you still can. Run to the lifeboat launching area and secure a place for you and your loved ones. There probably is food, water, blankets, and a radio to call for help. You can be rescued and return to safety.

As you can see from the sinking ship scenario, change occurs depending on the story you tell yourself. You will either linger on the boat or flee quickly to the "unknown" in the lifeboats. Although your automatic reaction comes first from the subconscious elephant brain, you can bypass that wiring with a new story that empowers you to take a different action. Both Christine's story about Mika and the sinking ship story make the point that change is hard. We are comfortable with what we know, and we have an inherent fear of the unknown. We also believe that understanding the story we are telling ourselves, to see whether it is empowering us to take the appropriate action, is important. And if it's not, the story can be nudged. In essence, although our brain connections (superhighways or dirt roads) are developed as we grow, they can be altered if we know how.

The Gift of Neuroplasticity—the Proof That We Can Grow and Adapt

Okay, so now we know four things: 1) The brain is a wonderful and complex tool, more quantum than mechanical; 2) We have two major periods in our lives when neurons fire and wire together; 3) We create superhighways and dirt roads of experience, knowledge, and connections; and 4) the brain is remarkably adaptable. It is true that learning and adapting during the two periods of growth are infinitely easier, as we all have seen young children learn a new language, zip by us on the ski slopes, and reprogram our smart phones that we can barely use. It is also true that our brains are not static, but dynamic tools that can be rewired to build new connections, learnings, and behaviors, and to reprogram the old.

Edward Taub, a renowned scientist from the University of Alabama, has done some startling research using what he calls C.I. or Constraint Induced Therapy. His research on how people can learn when they have lost one of their functions, be it brain or body, is pretty remarkable. He shows us that by using something he calls "massed practice," you can help rewire your brain by "triggering plastic changes" (qtd. in Doidge 149). According to Taub, we can pretty much change anything we want if we have the right motivation, process, and focus on making the change.

The good news about neuroplasticity, or the ability for

your brain to change/re-wire, is that your brain can be adaptable and flexible. Dr. Norman Doidge, in *The Brain That Changes Itself*, illustrates this with the following story:

> When a child learns to play piano scales for the first time, he tends to use his whole upper body—wrist, arm, and shoulder—to play each note. Even the facial muscles tighten into a grimace. With practice the budding pianist stops using irrelevant muscles and soon uses only the correct finger to play the note. He develops a "lighter touch," and if he becomes skillful, he develops "grace" and relaxes when he plays. (67)

Mihaly Csikszentmihalyi, cofounder of Positive Psychology, has labeled this effortless execution as "Flow." We can create new neural networks through practice, repetition, emotion, and hard work. These become superhighways that seem effortless to travel on and are much different than our dirt roads or the things we do not do well.

However, this very gift of plasticity is a curse as well because it also means our brains can be rigid and stagnant. Even if the highway we have built over the years takes us to the wrong place, or continuously has us falling off a cliff and hurting ourselves, or worse yet, hurting others, it is still the superhighway we know, and it is much easier to travel than the dirt road we don't know. Doidge calls this effect the "plastic paradox," stating that "the same neuroplastic properties that allow us to change our brains and produce more flexible behaviors can also allow us to produce more rigid ones" (242).

Since Christine and I believe in the almost unlimited potential of human beings to adapt, change, and grow, we choose to look at the glass as half-full. Neuroplasticity means we can adapt and create strong neural networks in our brains that lead us to excellence and doing things in the *flow*. But how do we *know* when to stay the same or pivot? This question reminds us of a story about Billy Carter, the much maligned brother of President Carter during his brother's presidency. Billy was meeting with a heart surgeon and a rocket scientist, and they were debating what they thought was the most important scientific discovery of all time. Of course, the rocket scientist said it was rocket propulsion, which had helped win a big war, send rockets into outer space, and explore the last frontier. How could that not be the most important? The heart surgeon retorted that with open heart surgery, he could open someone up, take out the person's living but damaged heart, and replace it with a new vibrant organ that would save and prolong the person's life. Pretty important stuff. Billy was quiet for a bit, and then he remarked, "Well, boys, I think it is the thermos jug." Both scientists laughed heartily and then asked, "Why would you say that?" Billy with a slow grin said, "Well, it keeps hot things hot and cold things cold." And then after an interminable pause, added, "But how does it *know*?"

When I first heard this, I thought, "Kind of funny, but what a dumb story." Yet as life went on, I started to realize how profound Billy's point was. How many times are we presented with data that is not so easy to synthesize and apply? How many times do we have conflicts in our schedules and want to do both, but we can't? How many times do we have big decisions such as: what college should I attend, what job should I take, or what city should we move to? We all know what it is like to be pulled in different directions by our elephant, which confuses the rider just enough to be unsure how to steer. If you slow down and observe this in your life, we think you will come to the same conclusion as Christine and I have: either Billy Carter was a really smart guy, or maybe this is just a really good story that makes a powerful point. It is often hard to know the right answer, right path, or correct action. How do we really *know*?

So our challenge with this gift of neuroplasticity is to figure out which behaviors help us accomplish the things we want to accomplish and why. Once we know that, we must tame the elephant and fire the new neurons often enough to make the highways we want the number one places to go, i.e., the superhighways. Plus, when you use the new highways over and over again: pay tolls, do maintenance, and upgrade them, the old highways atrophy, get forgotten, and lose the magic hold they once had. With a conscious process, focus, and practice, we can create superhighways that help us unleash our potential.

Figure 1.6

Even if they are currently dirt roads from our previous growth periods, we can now begin to use the dirt road, improving on it little by little every time we use it. Eventually, over time, it can become one of our new superhighways. Then, with the continuous use of this new superhighway and new neurons wiring and firing together, our old highway will fall into disrepair. The cement will crack, weeds will sprout, and pretty soon it will not be as attractive an option for us to follow. In effect, we have rewired our brains to create new behaviors that serve us well and help us accomplish the things we want in life. With determination, practice, and a few little Nudges, we can each unleash all of the potential with which we have been blessed. Christine and I are driven by these insights, and we believe we can facilitate your understanding and application of these insights by providing you with a powerful communication framework to use.

Before we continue our story about how we arrived at The Art of the Nudge™, there is another important concept we need to explain about the brain and "taking action," and how our conscious and subconscious mind lead us to do certain things.

The Event/Feelings/Action Cycle—and Our Subconscious Tells a Story

Before the innovation of new fMRI (functional magnetic resonance imaging) technology to study brain activity, neuroscientists and psychologists were studying the brain forensically with people who had experienced significant head trauma. Although this technique did lead to a lot of understanding, it does not compare to the leaps we have made with fMRI. We can compare this fMRI technology to many other technological innovations, such as the automobile, space flight, computers, the Internet, and smart phones. Most of the inventors and early adopters of those technologies could not even begin to imagine the huge implications and effects they would have on current theories, but these technologies made tectonic shifts anyway.

Just like the invention of the automobile or Internet, existing knowledge and cultural ideas were added to or debunked based on new discoveries that the specific technology facilitated. In the case of fMRI, the prevailing thought had been that when an *event* occurred, it caused an *emotion* in our amygdala (an area of the limbic/subconscious brain) that was transmitted to our conscious brain, or neocortex, and as a result of this signal, caused us to take an *action*. If we stop and think about this cycle, it makes a lot of sense. Most of us can think of things that have happened to us that seemingly occurred in exactly this manner. At least that is what we, and most others who studied this concept, thought at the time (D. Smith 110-111).

However, due to the new and growing knowledge base resulting in the use of fMRI technology, something very important has been discovered about what is *really* happening in the brain concerning the Event/Feelings/Action Cycle. The fMRI allows for more detailed information about all of the electrical firing going on with the connected neurons in our subconscious brain. Remember that we have about 100 billion neurons making ten to fifteen thousand connections— complex, quantum, and happening at lightning speed.

As we have mentioned before, the subconscious part of our brain contains the limbic center, and this stores all of our autobiographical history: everything that has happened to us, everything we have perceived, and even stuff that has just been told to us. It is not a well-organized Oracle Relational Database, but a very messy set of neural connections firing instantaneously and reacting to an event or information we receive. Our limbic center processes all of this input, links it to relevant networks, and makes heads or tails of the information, actually telling us a lot about the input.

Since the detailed brain maps from fMRIs can see the electrical impulses, we now know there is an added step in the Event/Feelings/Action Cycle. The added step is that our subconscious brain actually tells us a story (D. Smith 111).

Figure 1.8

All of this data coming in to the limbic center in the subconscious brain is synthesized, processed, and becomes a story that relates both the event and data occurring in the now with everything that has been captured in the past. The story it creates tells us how we should react to the event or stimuli. At the most basic level, think again about "fight or flight." Should I run because the scary dog is chasing me, or should I hold my ground and defend myself against the potential attack? On a more complex level, think about the following story of me as an eight-year-old boy and my experience with broccoli….

I was at Thanksgiving at my uncle's house, and my dad made me eat brown, yucky broccoli. It tasted so awful to my eight-year-old taste buds. Not only did I almost throw up, but I was so embarrassed as all of my older cousins laughed and made fun of me. That evening while I was lying in bed, my brain told itself that not only would I never eat broccoli again, but I might do bodily harm to anyone who even suggested it. This story that my subconscious brain created is the real reason I hated this vegetable for such a long time. However, when I found out that broccoli is considered a "superfood," my brain created a new story that shifted my thinking enough to retry broccoli and fall in love with this healthy vegetable. Can you remember an incident like this in your own life? I imagine that without thinking too hard, you can relate to some emotional event that occurred early in your life, colored your perception, and controls, to some extent, how you act now. Is the story you have locked in your brain true? Does it empower you to grow? Does it unleash your unfulfilled potential? Or does it limit you to a stagnant version of yourself?

Daniel Ariely and Daniel Kahneman (recipient of the 2002 Noble Prize in Economics) have done exceptional research on a controversial subject called behavioral economics. They show that although we all want to act rationally and do rational things, we don't. Some of the experiments they have conducted on how Princeton and Yale students make economic decisions are legendary. Their research explains why we all see an accident somewhat differently and why an "eyewitness account" is often not what really happened. It explains why we all "lie" a little bit, according to the other person's point of view, why smart people do dumb things, and why addicts repeat the same mistakes over and over again. Christine and I know this all sounds pretty bleak unless you, like us, believe in the almost unlimited potential of people, combined with the theory of neuroplasticity, and the power you have to create new stories, which help you pave new superhighways and enable the atrophy of current ones.

The Art of Nudging

Our belief about the untapped potential of people coupled with the new developments and understandings in brain science spurred Christine and I on to find a better way to help people unlock this potential. After years of work in real-world leadership and change situations with our clients, we realized a couple of things about our current world—The New Normal if you will. We seem to be moving faster. People are usually pressed for time, always in a hurry to get to the next meeting. Priorities shift instantly, and we spend our time multitasking, never quite finishing one thing before bouncing to the next. Compound this with the bombardment of digital and social media, stimuli that cause us to defocus, and you have a pretty harried and stressed world without the time or energy really to make human connections and get the whole story.

These current global conditions inspired us to try something radical. What if we took the approach that to speed up, you actually had to slow down? I mean, isn't there a fable where the turtle wins the race? What if instead of asking people to make large changes or quantum leaps, we could meet them where they are and give them a Nudge? No, not a noogie, but a small, encouraging way to get them to take the next logical step for them, building on success and change. What if we came up with a methodology that incorporated all we learned from psychology and brain science about humans and change, and we crafted something to harness those principles in a way that is extremely usable by ordinary people? Well, we have!

We came up with a theory that we tested over and over. We found time and time again that it was counterintuitive, and although you might get initial pushback, it worked more often than not. We found out that people loved to slow down and figure out their "Why." We also observed that when people really understood their Why, they were more committed to taking decisive action. They would start to make their own small nudges to shift habits, behaviors, and actions. Most people can relate to a time when they have been told what to do by someone else—a parent, a boss, a spouse, a sibling—without a clear purpose. Many of us fought it. Our subconscious brain was screaming, "I do not want to do this! Why am I wasting my time?" How did this make you feel? Now think about a time when you knew your own Why, so you chose decisive actions that you would and could take to tackle the project. How did you feel when you had this direction? We think you know the answer to this, as well as which of these tactics effective leaders use more frequently.

With these two different approaches to influencing behavior in mind, Christine and I spent time codifying what we were doing and then re-testing, repeating, and evaluating. We continued to research topics related to human behavior and change, communication theory, leadership, brain science, and behavioral economics until we were ready to share our communication framework. You are reading about the research and consulting we did to tie all of these subjects together—subjects about who we are, how and why we really make decisions and do the things we do, and why we find comfort in some things and not in others. As we continued to work with people on how to improve their performance and the performance of their organizations, we devised a process to pull this all together and help us make small nudges that can have quantum effects. We also borrowed several existing tools that support the framework: personality profiles; the concept of story, both story gathering and telling; and the idea of taking small steps or Nudges.

So we don't get too far ahead of ourselves, let us first define the concept of the "Nudge." I had an excellent communications professor while completing my Executive MBA studies at Emory University in Atlanta. One of the many memorable things this professor said was, "The natural outcome of two people communicating is confusion because I do not speak very well and I do not listen very well." So let us clarify the definition of NUDGE so you understand what we mean. The Merriam-Webster Dictionary defines "nudge" in several ways:

- To touch or push (someone or something) gently;
- To encourage (someone) to do something;
- To prod lightly, urge into action.

So this is what we mean by Nudge, with an emphasis on "gently" and "lightly." A recent example of this concept of "Nudging" someone is when I relearned to play the guitar. I started playing as a senior in college, was never very good, and ultimately gave it up. I was inspired during a trip to Germany while visiting my oldest son, to try again. My son, who is quite accomplished on the guitar, asked me, "Dad, why don't you pick it up and start playing again?" He also recommended a website for easy songs and a chord book that would teach the fundamentals of chords and notes.

It sounded cool and fun, so I began the journey, trying to play for twenty minutes every day. Then I hit a pothole. Those damn dirt roads have those you know. The song in the book was unknown to me and too hard. I couldn't get it and played poorly. Yes, it was a dirt road. Yes, my elephant took me back to the superhighway: "You don't play the guitar. You don't know that song, and you are really not that good anyway. Just stop." So I was stuck for a couple of days until I called my son. After I relayed my problem to him rather sheepishly, he replied, "Dad, don't worry about that. When I am stuck, I actually write the notes above the chord in the songbook, then back up and play it very slowly. After a couple of times, it starts coming to me."

Brilliant nudge. Instead, my son could have responded, "Dad, are you kidding me? I thought you wanted to play the guitar. You went to West Point and were an army ranger. Don't you have enough discipline or self-confidence to fiddle with a songbook in your own house?" Now, although all of that is true, I am so thankful he had the sense to nudge me instead; otherwise, what would I likely have done with statement number two? Most certainly, the reaction would have been a limbic one, an amygdala hijack. Angry, upset, and just plain disgusted, I would have quit playing. However, thanks to my son's nudge, I took the next logical step.

Think about how many times you or your associates have been stuck. What did you get or give? Was it a nudge, or some offensive jab to the ego, creating tension and friction that reinforced the old story: *"Man, do not take that dirt road. It is too hard to pave over and you already know about those stupid potholes. You have this superhighway already in place. I mean, it doesn't take you where you want to go, but it's easy. It will be a fun ride, and there aren't any obstacles. Let's stick with that."* I don't know about you, but Christine and I have not been so gentle with ourselves and others at times, and certainly in our own careers and consulting work, we have seen leaders who were very right and oh, so ineffective because they used aggressive pushes vs. nudges.

We are not criticizing because we know these folks either let their elephants respond emotionally, or they just did not understand how to flex to meet other people's needs. I mean, their elephants are raring to go and their brain is telling them that when they speak to other people, they should just appear logical and rational. When they are direct and clear, others will get it immediately and change at once. What if I told you, "Change is easy, and if you just tell someone what to do, he will change right away and shift to follow you"?

Is that statement logical and rational to you? It is to us. But guess what? It rarely works. As a matter of fact, we can each think of times when we were oh, so right, and oh, so fast, but unfortunately, ineffective in convincing others. Most of the time, it is just easier to tell other people what to do, right? However, now that we know all of this powerful stuff, Christine and I use our own process and tools to increase effectiveness and performance even with ourselves.

So now that you understand what we mean by Nudge and why we think it is critical to high performance, achieving our potential, and taking Action, hopefully you can opt into using it. We are sharing the current neuroscience in order to help you think differently about your brain and its potential. We know we have more potential to achieve and to accomplish things we want to do, and we know change is hard. We believe that if you learn to use our communication framework and the tools that go along with it, it will become easier to take Action and achieve powerful results. So here it is!

The Art of the NUDGE™ Framework (TATN):

1. N - (K)now what you want to do or accomplish, and most importantly, WHY?
2. U - Understand the current story being told by you and others in your organization.
3. D - Develop a new story that empowers people and ignites their passion to take Action.
4. G - Give and tell this story often enough to inspire others to act with their maximum potential.
5. E - Evaluate progress, celebrate success, and continue to Nudge or adapt.

In the next chapter, we will introduce you to the other two tools we mentioned, besides nudging, that support this framework: Personality Profiles and Story. Then we will cover each step in detail, showing you how and when to follow the step and use the tools for impressive NUDGES.

Chapter Reflections

1. People and organizations have untapped potential to grow and achieve.
   - Change is hard.
   - We believe you have to slow down to speed up and use Nudges to inspire Action.

2. Taking the time to understand current revelations in the science of the brain and how the brain works is critical to helping you achieve better personal and organizational results.

   - Our brains consist of a triune, layered brain and our left/right brain.
   - Our conscious and subconscious areas of the brain are like an iceberg.
   - We can learn to integrate these areas more effectively.

3. Understanding the power of the brain:

   - We make significant connections during two major growth periods in our lifetime. Neuroplasticity of the brain shows that we can learn to rewire these connections and adapt.
   - Superhighways represent familiar roads our brains have traveled that cause us, subconsciously, to repeat behaviors—whether they are "functional" or "dysfunctional."
   - Dirt Roads represent less traveled pathways of the brain that allow you to unleash potential. You travel these pathways when adapting and changing.
   - We have an elephant and a rider driving these roads. The elephant represents our limbic brain that allows emotional reactions

to rule our behavior. The Rider represents our aware, less evolved brain—the neocortex—that takes decisive action versus simply reacting or maintaining the status quo.

- Understanding and practice allow the rider to control our elephant and turn dirt roads into new superhighways.

4. The modern world is working against us with the rapid pace of change and advances in communication technology.

- There seems to be less time in our day.
- Our priorities change very quickly.
- We are bombarded with stimuli from many sources that cause stress and often result in us reacting versus acting.

5. Slowing down is counterintuitive but actually allows you to move faster, getting better results.

- Understanding our own and others' stories is a key to inspiring action.
- Current brain science confirms that our subconscious brain is already telling us an existing story based on our well-formed connections. *Events/(Story)/Feelings/Action Cycle.*
- Harnessing our untapped potential necessitates everyone taking his or her own action, rather than being directed or told…. We call

this a Nudge.

- We believe that once you understand the current story, you can develop a new, more inspiring story that can lead to more action.

6. The Art of the Nudge (TATN) is our communication framework created to help people realize personal and organizational potential. It is a roadmap with tools to assist in continuous improvement and innovation, creating action for specific personal and business outcomes. *N. U. D. G. E.*

Nudges

1. Ask yourself, "How much of my potential am I realizing?" Most people use only a small portion of their brain power. Think of a reason you would want to utilize more of this potential of your brain.
2. To teach is to learn. Try explaining to a colleague or a friend why you now believe we all have untapped potential that can help us achieve and grow.
3. Reflect on a time when you regretted your actions or words—when you let your raging elephant take control of your rider. What were you thinking and feeling in the moment versus when you calmed down? Did your reaction help or

hurt you toward getting results? Do you wish
you would have handled this differently, and
what specifically would you have done?

Chapter 2

Why Personality Profiles and Story Are Essential Tools to Knowing the Right Nudge

Early in Christine's career when she was being trained as a therapist, she was talking with her mentor, Andy, about a family she was working with that was repeating the same dysfunctional behavior. This is her story:

> I couldn't seem to convince the parents that repeating their destructive behavior was having serious consequences on their child's emotional well-being and development. I was sharing my frustration with Andy about how it was so obvious that the parents' behavior was ultimately hurting themselves and their child. In my growing exasperation, I asked, "How is it that they can't see this, and why can't I convince

them to change their approach?" Andy wisely responded, "Christine, most often people start a behavior for a perfectly good and functional reason. It is only when this same behavior is continued with no functional effect that the behavior shifts from being functional to dysfunctional." He continued, "Unfortunately, it is not obvious to people when they are no longer getting the same payoff for their behavior. If it was obvious, they would be more likely to stop it. The problem is that we are just not that good at knowing ourselves. If we don't know why we ourselves are doing some things and not others, then never mind us trying to understand and adapt to other people." Andy really got me thinking about how hard it is to understand who we are and what we want.

Understanding all of those neurons, all of the connections—the superhighways and dirt roads—and all that is stored in that magnificent brain is daunting. Assuming that we do not know ourselves, how can we ever understand others?

Some psychologists categorize all of this information and these connections as being part of our "core personality"; we have life experiences, values, and memories that reside in our limbic brain, and we also have things both internal and external that are motivating us right now. We know these all reside in our elephant and our rider, and people have used some powerful tools over the years to aid in understanding each of these. We use three—Personality Profiles, Story, and Nudges—to help us execute the Steps of TATN. We will describe these tools because we believe they are important, simple, and easily applicable. Picture the TATN Framework as the car, with Personality Profiles as the tires; Story as the engine; and Nudges as the gas pedal. After a brief introduction of what they are, we will then describe the Five-Step TATN Communication Framework and how to apply these tools in each step.

Nature vs. Nurture Becomes Nature AND Nurture

Before introducing the tools, we want to reinforce our tipping point. Instead of thinking of nature vs. nurture or mind over matter, we think of AND. Instead of speeding up to respond to the myriad of digital stimuli, we slow down. Instead of asking ourselves or others to make large shifts, we Nudge. These are the core ideas of the TATN Framework that we can harness to unleash more of our untapped potential, when we know how. And the tools we will describe here support the execution of the communication framework.

When we reflect on current brain science, it's apparent we already know a lot. We can most likely agree that nature is what we are born with. Many of those neurons were wiring and firing inside the womb. How we interacted with the outside world inside that safe, warm place may have influenced us as well. How

71

much? No one is really sure. But we do know that we have all been born with certain inherent characteristics and traits. We call this "personality" and believe it was fundamentally shaped very early in life. The other parts of nature influenced by nurture are those two high-growth periods when the neurons are making trillions of connections.

We know these periods are influenced by our environments, cultures, experiences, human interactions, and reinforcements. Although the brain is doing a lot of the work under the surface—the submerged iceberg— we are certainly interacting with our world to make conscious choices on what we do, like, what to spend time on, and gravitate toward. Why are some people aggressive and why do they want to control and dominate, while others are more reserved and just want to blend in? Why can some of us meet new people easily and make friends quickly, while others hang in the background? Why are some of us very precise and detailed while others are more conceptual? Why do some love playing the piano while others like sports? Why are some interested in math and science while others prefer music and art?

We believe that these categories fall into personalities, life experiences, and motivations, sometimes not easily seen or understood. What if we could better understand this development of nature and nurture in ourselves and others? Might it help us know the right Nudges to take to get what we want, adapting ourselves in a better way to empower others to grow and take action? Christine and I have sought to understand the development of nature and nurture to do precisely that.

Why Personality Profiles Can Help Us Understand Ourselves and Others

The history of personality profiles goes back to 444 BC. The two most widely known psychologists of this discipline in our western world are Carl Jung and William Marston. Their theories stem from the Greek physician Hippocrates' sorting of earth, wind, fire, and water as the basic elements that affect our personalities. Many personality profile tools are on the market today: Meyers Briggs, PI, DiSC, and Kolbe that deliver a productive and useful assessment of core personality.

Christine has seen the use of these tools in psychological services environments. She and I have both used them in the corporate world in hiring situations, sales situations, leadership development, collaboration with teams, and conflict resolution. We know that although we all have a basic personality type, we can continue to adapt, flex, and grow to meet others where they are to be more effective. However, to do this, we need to know our own personality, as well as the other's personality. That is, the characteristics of each and how to flex our styles for more effective interaction and communication. We believe that whatever personality tool you use, it will deliver some positive and impactful insights on your understanding of yourself and others, and we encourage the use of a consistent tool organizationally to develop a common language and dialogue. These tools will help us understand the personality we and others have developed through nature, nurture, and the brain, and they can certainly be a guide for how both to communicate and Nudge more effectively.

Recently, Christine and one of our sales reps, Jess, were starting a large project with a new prospective client. They had developed a strong relationship with John, the new Senior VP and the main buyer/decision maker. Jess and Christine had crafted a proposal for him to deliver an intervention that precisely met his core Nudge, with metrics included to measure the outcomes: increased lease sales, thereby increasing revenue and profitability; increased customer touch for lease customers to be retained for multiple product cycles, boosting revenue and reducing cost of sales; and an increased inventory of well-maintained and high-end used cars for additional sales with new customers, increasing revenue, profit, and customer potential.

Jess and Christine felt confident in their efforts and knew that John would read it and sign immediately. Uh-oh… When one week dragged to two, Jess got very impatient and frustrated with John. He was thinking, "Why did he cancel our meeting? Why wasn't he getting back to us? What was wrong?" And, of course, Jess wanted to take decisive and possibly aggressive action by calling John immediately to find this out.

Since Christine understands the "slow down to speed up" idea, she recommended that instead of calling right away, they look at John's personality profile and compare it to Jess's profile. Yes, they knew him very well, and Christine analyzed people professionally, but why not take ten minutes to use an existing and objective tool? So they did a compare report on Jess's personality and John's personality, and found one key that directed them to a more appropriate way to interact than Jess's initial reaction. What they learned was that yes, John was driven and action-oriented like Jess; however, John was much more reflective and needed more time to analyze and make decisions. Once he made a decision, he was ALL IN and drove it hard, but he just may not be as quick as Jess initially on making the decision.

So instead of phoning John directly and potentially not meeting him where he was, the Nudge was to request a face-to-face meeting with John to go over the proposal in detail. Christine would conduct most of the discussion because she would implement the project and knew all of the intricate details, and Jess would take a supporting role and interject, where needed, on the value. The details of that meeting are not the point. The point is that even with someone we thought we knew well, taking a little more time and using an objective, research-based tool, helped us come up with a different action step. Slowing down to speed up helped create a more intentional action, rather than an impulsive reaction; the rider was steering the elephant.

We could continue with many stories of how using a tool like this with leaders, salespeople, and teams added some terrific insight that made a difference, and we highly recommend personality assessments as an integral part of TATN. If you are dealing with complex deal situations, high-potential people, or situations with high risk and high reward, why would you not slow down, taking a little more time to use an available and proven tool, and possibly get a more effective NUDGE to speed up?

Although Christine and I have used and been trained on many of these tools, when an organization does not have one, we recommend Everything DiSC from Wiley Publishing. We use Everything DiSC because of the strong research and Computer Adaptive Testing behind it. This tool is simple to understand, and the advanced online experience makes it easy to use. In particular, the technology allows for easy access to profiles and useful comparisons between individuals and groups, both internally in leadership and management situations, and externally with clients in sales and customer service situations. Whatever personality assessment you use, DiSC or other, these tools can provide an objective insight into personalities that will aid you immensely in deciphering at least this part of the puzzle. Now that we have discussed the usefulness of personality profiles, let us move on to the other tool we actively use to better understand our life experience, values, motivations, and biases: Story.

Why Story Works

"Once upon a time...."

Does this phrase take you back to a different time, perhaps in your childhood? What is your favorite childhood story? *Alice in Wonderland, Goldilocks and the Three Bears, Goodnight Moon*? Do these stories make you want to curl up in front of a warm fireplace with a blanket... relaxed, unstressed, and ready to learn? We think Story elicits this response because it is how we record our life journey, and it is also how our brain operates.

Research on Story history tells us that stories were first recorded on cave drawings some 95,000 years ago. You can visit caves in France and Portugal to see the amazing adventures of our ancestors who were struggling to talk. There are stories of wonderful hunts where animals were killed to bring food home to feed the tribe. There are celebrations of children being born and making rites of passage. There are stories of heroic events as well as tragedies. There are stories of rulers, subjects, and, of course, death. Why did our ancestors tell these stories? What were they for? Who read the cave wall drawings? What happened after that?

Story was used to pass down culture. It was how younger tribe members learned new things. Through the use of story, they saw and got new ideas of what to do, not to do, and what improvements to make. Story was the way to pass things down over time, make things immortal, and brand thoughts and ideas into our hearts and minds. "Studying old stories is not only for the benefit of historians, or for understanding the way our ancestors thought. These stories have their own power" (Sedlacek 4). Anthropologists confirm that the three oldest civilizations known to man—Sumerian, Hebrew, and Greek—all told stories in several ways.

Yes, in the early days, we wrote on cave walls, but as language developed, we began to tell these stories around campfires to our fellow tribesman, children, grandchildren, and other relatives. Eventually, we began to write and put stories down on paper so they could be shared more widely. Gutenberg's invention of the printing press accelerated this development resulting in millions of books of stories that you can read for enjoyment and learning, and, of course, the Internet and our digital society have revolutionized this capability. As young kids, we used these magical instruments, called stories, to become somebody else. They helped us break free from our current environment for the time being and let our mind and subconscious brain take us to places virtually unknown to our real bodies. When a story captured our imagination, we got in the *flow* and became lost to reality. Storytelling is powerful stuff we have certainly all experienced as we truly became the Hero of the story. Benjamin Carson, the renowned pediatric neurosurgeon, relates in his book how the stories he read as a young boy and man transported him from the dreary reality of his very poor family and single mother. They allowed him to dream of different ideas and circumstances, and they played a large part in helping him see and create a different world for himself and his family. So *why* does Story work?

Why Story Is the Right Engine

Okay, so stories have been around a lot longer than maybe you knew or thought. And, yes, you know a lot about stories and even like them. In fact, you are probably a good storyteller, at least for stories you know well or have experienced personally. The main point is that the most powerful part of our brain, the subconscious, records information in story. The elephant, our limbic center, loves to hear, remember, and tell stories. Every story we have been told or read is stored in some form or fashion inside the elephant, and we draw upon this information effortlessly and instantaneously, even if it is not factually correct.

By contrast, our neocortex likes facts and figures. And didn't that famous Greek philosopher/scientist Aristotle tell us that we should all be logical and rational? To be emotional was foolish; only people without knowledge relied on emotions. Aristotle also believed that the sun revolved around the earth. Obviously, he did not have a telescope or fMRI technology, and he did not know that the rider was often hijacked by the more powerful elephant. So he tried to convince people with facts, figures, and other data that appealed to their logical minds or neocortexes. Appealing to logic has a couple of problems, however, as neuroscientists know today.

The first problem is that this slower logical brain processes things linearly, and it can only process so much information at once. Remember my famous communications professor from Emory? Well, he taught another memorable theory called 3/5/7/9. The idea behind this theory is that when you are speaking to people and you present three ideas or messages, 90 percent of the audience will remember them. If you present five messages, it drops dramatically to 50 percent remembering them. Seven messages is still worse—only 30 percent of the people will remember, and finally, nine.... Well, as they say in Brooklyn, "Fuhgeta-bout-it." Retention goes to 10 percent for the listeners. If this theory is correct, it tells us that trying to influence someone with a lot of facts and figures may not be the best way to do it. If you have to present facts and figures, use the memorable number of three and wrap those in a story to make your point better.

The second problem with relying on logic and reason to influence others is that our logical, analytical neocortex is also the part of our brain that is skeptical, and for many of us engineers, sometimes cynical. So here is a great idea: Let's try to convince someone to go down this new dirt road vs. his or her already established superhighway by presenting a lot of facts and figures to prove to his or her challenging, skeptical mind that we are so smart and so right. This does work, sometimes.

But those of us who have sat through the boring PowerPoint presentations we discussed earlier know that it may not be the best way. Christine tells a story that brings this point home.

After a few years of doing clinical assessments, I began working with an Employee Assistant Program, where we consulted with over a 100 different organizations and industries: banking, technology, hospitals, government agencies, QVC, you name it. I was excited for my new career adventure, in part, because I had the opportunity to go out and speak to and train people at all levels of organizations to help them improve and grow. However, I had never conducted training before; I had not experienced working with organizations, and, consequently, I was pretty terrified to get up and speak in the front of the room. I mean, who was going to take me seriously at twenty-seven years of age? How would I convince them I knew what I was talking about?

I started working closely with my boss, following him around from place to place, and watching him conduct the workshops I would soon be tasked to conduct myself. It was fun to see him in action, and he was very engaging as he told stories to make his point and help people learn the lessons. This all took place at a time before laptop computers and PowerPoint projectors. In fact, the flipchart was the only real prop. And yes, I have now revealed that I am no longer twenty-seven.

Anyway, for that first year, I literally copied everything my boss did. I copied his mannerisms, used the same voice inflections, and told his stories, as I didn't have any stories of my own yet. I learned that I did possess some commanding platform skills. As I continued for the next three years, I increased my repertoire of stories, and I learned over and over again that the key to success in front of people was all about keeping the audience from getting bored.

Suddenly, my career came to a screeching halt when I went out on disability the next year due to my auto accident. I still remember the day I came back to work and met with the training coordinator, Nancy, to get acclimated to the changes that had occurred when I was out. Nancy sat me down in the conference room and showed me this thing she called a PowerPoint projector, and how all the trainings were now done using PowerPoint and a computer. "This is how we train people now," she said. I remember looking at her and saying, "You're kidding me, right? You mean I have to put up all that I'm going to say, bullet point by bullet point, as I say it?" Nancy replied, "Yep, this is what people want; the world is computerized now."

I remember thinking, *This is absolutely crazy.* However, I was a good, loyal employee, so I was bound and determined to try this new way, if it was what people wanted. So even though my visceral reaction that communicating with people this way was crazy, I became part of the PowerPoint movement and slowly, but surely, I was designing trainings bullet point by bullet point as well. As I look back at the ten-plus years I spent being part of the madness, I reflect on the words my mentor, Andy, told me about functional behavior becoming dysfunctional.... Maybe there was a logical reason for why PowerPoint started. Maybe there was a rationale I never got that would explain why this was a good reason in the first place, and I just missed it. All I know is that even though I sat through the boredom, pain, and ineffectiveness of those presenting with PowerPoint, bullet point by bullet point, I allowed my own behavior to tip into this same dysfunction. Fortunately, as luck would have it, I always told stories along with those mind-numbing slides. With our work over the last few years, I now make critical points only through stories because it just plain works.

Okay, so what if we cannot totally get away from PowerPoint or plain facts? What about wrapping some of those facts in a story? Does your neocortex relax when someone says, "Can I tell you a quick story?" How does this reaction compare to, "Please turn your attention to bullet point fifteen on slide 792?" Yuck! There is an old Jewish teaching story that goes something like this…. "Truth, naked and cold, had been turned away from every door in the village" when she met her friend Parable. They talked together and combined their strengths to go out to tell the story again, and were welcomed at every table in the village (Simmons 27).

Most people only remember three things in the neocortex, but that powerful quantum limbic brain can remember the whole story—all the truths wrapped up in the parable. And not only that, the elephant *likes* to hear stories. It welcomes them, stores them, and repeats them. So you might understand why Christine and I use Story for the Engine in our The Art of The Nudge™ Communication Framework, and how it helps us better understand ourselves and others. We both learned and used story firsthand, and we have been teaching story to others for the last three years, experiencing the difference in action and reaction with this tool. We have firsthand knowledge of both the power of this skill, particularly compared with the sleep-inducing alternative: presenting page after page of boring detailed facts. Trust us on this and see who else does it.

Who Has Used Story?

If story is a more effective way of communicating, which leaders or powerful influencers have used it to harness the strength of people and achieve big results? This should be the shortest paragraph in the book because each one of us can think of a myriad of effective leaders who have used this tool: Jesus, Lincoln, and Martin Luther King, Jr. for beginners. And yes, also how about some terrible ones: Hitler, Stalin, or Kim Jong-il? We can all probably think of other leaders or influencers in our lives who have made their points with stories, pictures, anecdotes, or metaphors, and most likely, this skill was more impactful than a long, detailed, factual speech. By the way, for our purposes, we are classifying all of these things under the headline of "Story" because they all create an emotional limbic response that leads to action.

We most likely all have favorite movies or books whose stories have moved us. Although facts are important, it is the emotional contexts that make us "feel" and remember. Besides, we have already learned that because our neurons fire and wire uniquely, our "facts" may differ from your "facts" based upon our past experiences, stored information, values, culture, and ability to listen. So whether these moving stories are 100 percent accurate or not may not matter, but what does matter is that they make a point, cause us to feel something, and lead us to take action, a Nudge.

One of my favorite motivational stories is the "Inch by Inch" speech by Al Pacino in the movie *Any Given Sunday*. Pacino plays the role of Tony D'Amato, a washed out NFL coach with a losing team. He is under pressure from the owner and players while losing a big game, and yet, he has the gall to give a pretty moving and vulnerable speech at halftime. It starts out personal and slow, making him real and vulnerable like the players. It moves to an analogy of football and life, inch by inch, and finally has them up yelling and screaming, motivated and ready to go out and beat the other team. What an inspiration that story provided. What powerful emotions it evoked. You will have to rewatch the film if you do not remember the ending.

There are countless stories—whether of sports, history, love, etc.—we relate to, remember, and allow to move us. How about Mel Gibson in *Braveheart*, a powerful story that resulted in freeing Scotland from the tyranny of the English? How could William Wallace take a ragtag, last minute gathering of Scottish clans, who held a lot of personal animosity, and get them to rout the much larger, well-trained English army? Can you remember him riding that horse, with his face painted and screaming, "Freedom!"?

We have seen many influential people in history, in our personal lives, and in books and movies use story. We have concluded that the main reason they do this is that it works. We believe this powerful skill has atrophied in our digital society, and that if more leaders and influencers learned how to use this skill professionally, they would be more effective. Most of you are probably thinking, "Well, they don't know me. I am a great storyteller. I use stories all the time and make all of my important points with them." And this is most likely partly accurate. But you may not be as effective as you think, and not as often as you remember.

In his book *Subliminal*, Leonard Mlodinow mentions an experiment that illustrates this point. A large population of engineers were asked to rate themselves by percentages, i.e., top 5 percent, top 10 percent, top 20 percent, etc. Interestingly enough, 30-40 percent of those professionals ranked themselves in the top 5 percent. Now, your left brain analytical side should be kicking in and asking, "How can that be?" If there are only 5 percent in the 5 percent how can 30-40 percent be in the top 5 percent? Good question. Mlodinow states, "Psychologists call this tendency for inflated self-assessment, the 'above-average effect'" (198). In other words, we rate ourselves higher than we might be because we could be good at it, we think we are good at it, and this is what we tell ourselves (remember the limbic brain).

The reason we bring this up is that there are some great storytellers in this world, and everyone has the ability to tell good stories. However, we have found that this critical skill to leading and inspiring people is usually not learned, developed, and practiced like a professional skill. Think about who the professional storytellers are in this world. We think that songwriters, movie directors, and novelists are among some of the best. Think about what they do before they get up on stage for the new Taylor Swift Tour, or how many cuts they take before a scene is really complete for *Unbroken*; or how many edits, rewrites, and re-edits occur for Grisham, Patterson, or J.K. Rowling. We only say this because we also believed we were in the top 5 percent of storytellers in the world, but when we started consciously using and practicing this skill, we found out that we, too, were average. However, by teaching and coaching others to develop this skill, we have gotten a lot better. And it has helped us make a bigger difference. If you believe in this skill, we are encouraging you to build on it as well. What stories are you telling now and what stories could you tell to inspire people to action?

Stories Do the Selling for Us

We have already mentioned that we include word pictures, images, metaphors, and anecdotes into our idea of "Story." We received a story from a very high-performing female software sales rep who attended one of our workshops. Robyn was getting married, and she was having a tense discussion with her in-laws about the rehearsal dinner. They lived out West and were a little shocked by New York City prices, but they also wanted to host a rehearsal dinner to honor their son and new daughter-in-law, and to entertain their family and guests well. The struggle was that the financial goal and entertainment goal were somewhat at odds with one another. Although the parents thought they knew what they wanted, they were astonished at the price.

Robyn, who is quite intuitive, grasped the power of story from the workshop and crafted a moving description of the two possible rehearsal dinner venues, using facts to provide a realistic contrast. Oh yeah, she did throw in a few emotions about how they might feel in the dark, dingy basement ballroom of the cheap place, compared to the wonderful feeling they would have being on the forty-third floor overlooking a stunning view of Manhattan in the more expensive venue. Since Robyn is an innovative top performer, a brilliant idea hit her. Instead of simply telling this story, why not live it? So when her future in-laws came to New York City, she took them to the first place and let them feel the dreariness themselves. Then she and her future in-laws met her parents for a fabulous dinner at the second place, stunning view and all, not to mention the incredible food and impeccable service.

In relaying all of this to us, she tried to convince us that she really didn't tell a story and did not even need her story. Of course, we know she absolutely not only told it, but she acted it out effectively, and I think we all know what the end result was. What we do not really know is why she didn't think of this first. Why wasn't this really smart superstar, who uses Customer Stories often, thinking of story naturally? Well, because it was a dirt road for her. Her original PowerPoint for the mother-in-law was filled with facts, figures, distances to hotels, cab fares, blah, blah, blah, blah, blah. Why did it take our Immersion Workshop for her to get it and start using this tool in conversations that mattered? All I can report is that she was ecstatic with the new approach, saying to me, "This is like selling without selling. I'll be using this method a lot when I need to be inspiring and get other people to take action to support our goals."

What Types of Stories Do We Need?

Now that we've shown why Story is important, who uses it, and a simple example of its power, let us shift gears and talk about what *types* of stories we may need to tell. Although we will later discuss a recommended Arsenal of Stories to share for different people in different roles, we think the best way to approach your story is to think about who you are telling it to first and foremost, and "Why" you are telling it. Now if you are just sitting around and relaxing with friends at a barbecue, go ahead and tell any old story. But if this is serious business and you are telling a story to influence people to action, you need to think about who they are, what is in their memory bank on their superhighway, who/what would they identify with, and what might the potholes be on their dirt road that we want to avoid. Of course, closely aligned with this thought is: Why are you telling this story? Just like in *Alice in Wonderland*, if you are not clear about where you are going, any story will take you there.

There are a lot of stories we can tell about life and our experiences. Every credible author we have read on Story: Annette Simmons, Mark Goulston, Joe Campbell,

Paul Smith, Peg Neuhauser, and Mike Bosworth has an Inventory of Stories for your arsenal. However, if we are trying to nudge someone to action, it has to be an inspiring, emotional story. You can definitely pull one of these from an Arsenal of Stories that makes your point, or craft a new one uniquely for the situation.

What thoughts are going through your head when you meet a new person? We usually are wondering who the person is, why he is here, and what he wants. Now, this is the neocortex speaking, of course. Our subconscious brain, on the other hand, is trying to figure out the fight or flight thing or whether or not we like this person and want to hang out. So it makes sense that all of us would need a story of who we are, why we do what we do, and of a company. These can be melded into one story or told separately. Remember to be aware of who you are telling the story to and the situation. Is it a new person at your golf club? Is it a new employee? Is it a new customer you are meeting? The situation is directly relevant to both how much is in your story and how long you tell it. We encourage people to build a good story that makes a point for either a specific person or category of persons. Once you have the right flow, facts, and emotions, and have practiced it enough to give it naturally and conversationally, we encourage you to deliver it in ninety seconds, three to five minutes, and up to twenty minutes—of course being sensitive to the interest, attention, and body language of the other person.

Everyone should have the three stories mentioned in the previous paragraph in his or her repertoire, and all of us should also have Customer Stories to relate to prospects. Is it not our intent for our customers to get into the story of the hero we are discussing; to let them see what the character is going through, to identify with the character because they have vicariously lived part of the story, and then want to become like that hero? Christine definitely listened to a golf pro relaying a story about another lady, who, immediately following his breakthrough advice, improved her handicap from a thirteen to a ten. If you are a leader in an organization, team, and/or family, we believe you should have a Vision and Strategy Story, along with a Culture Story. After all, a famous book claims, "Where there is no vision, the people perish...." (The Bible, Proverbs 29:18, KJV).

Most of us will certainly need stories about lessons we have learned. I mean how else can we help prevent people from making the same dumb mistakes we have made? Of course, the normal response is, "Just tell them not to do that." Okay, we all know at this stage in the book that just because we know the right answer and have seen the same mistake before, simply telling someone not to do something may not work. Remember the elephant progressing down the superhighway that it knows, the fear of change and the unknown, and simply the fact that most people do not like to be told what to do, especially after the age of fourteen.

So how about we say, instead, "Let me tell you a story," and tell the person about someone else who went through a similar situation, or made a mistake. Your intended audience's members don't have to know the character in the story, but they do need to identify with them. What if they feel the gloom in the bad thing that happened, or the thrill of the good thing? Might their subconscious brains store this great story and pull it up the next time they are in similar situations? That is what that quantum fast brain does. It takes those associations and relates them so we tell ourselves a new story, feel something, and then take action. All of our empirical and non-empirical evidence leads us to believe that these Lessons Learned Stories are much more effective than just telling someone what to do.

Yes, we know that it seems faster and easier to tell people what to do, and harder and a little bit longer to tell a story. We have observed, however, that telling people what to do creates resistance. Embracing an emotional and powerful story, instead, allows them to opt in and take Action. In essence, slow down to speed up. The Art of the Nudge.

If you are a business person, we highly recommend Paul Smith's book *Lead with a Story*. In this book, Smith explains that Procter and Gamble has one of the best corporate training programs in America, and that they train their leaders on how to tell stories. Smith gives examples of stories for a myriad of leadership and management situations that are practical and adaptable. Christine and I think we touch most of these with the following categories of stories:

1. Vision Stories and Strategy Stories
2. Culture Stories
3. Company Stories
4. Customer Stories
5. Why I Do What I Do Stories
6. Lessons Learned Stories

Why Story Gathering Is More Important Than Telling

A huge movement is afoot in the U.S. for people to go back to their roots and relearn and practice the powerful skill of storytelling. Because we are in the Leadership Development and Sales Training business, we believe that only about 5 percent of business people in the U.S. have been given the opportunity to learn and practice this skill. Yes, they can all know how to tell stories, but do they have a map, and/or do they really know what makes up a good story? Have they practiced giving their stories as many times as a famous musician has practiced his song sets for a big tour? We are not sure whether you have, but we hope this book nudges you to get more interested in this skill. It is a powerful engine that inspires Nudges.

There are two sides to Story, and we believe Telling is less important. The more important skill, Story Gathering, can lead to unbelievable results. If you use Telling, you will most likely have more influence and make a bigger difference than other people. However, if you learn Gathering and do it well, it will be like you have *magical powers*! Now, I can imagine that you think we are being a little melodramatic and over the top, but what if we are right? Annette Simmons, a renowned author on storytelling inadvertently recognizes the power of Gathering. She writes, "My own experience teaching story telling as an influence strategy, has taught me the importance of listening to someone's old story before I try to introduce a new one" (184). In *Just Listen*, Mark Goulston writes, "Inside every person, no matter how important or famous, is a real person who needs to 'feel felt.' Satisfy that need and you'll transform yourself from a face in the crowd to an ally or friend" (53). Maybe there is something here.

Story Gathering is a skill that is dramatically underutilized. Remember the fast pace of change in our digital society, and the bombardments from social media and mobile communication? We have no time to get all of these important things done. This lack of time drives us to respond immediately in a Telling fashion, feeling like there is no time for Gathering. How would we ever have time to sit down and listen to someone and gather his or her story? Not happening; I have too much to do. I am too busy to harness human potential in any other way than a direct, logical, Telling approach. Huh?

The problem with this response, as you know, is that 80 billion of those neurons and a lot of those networks live in "limbic land." How did that elephant get so big again?

"Social connection is such a basic feature of human experience that when we are deprived of it, we suffer" (Mlodinow, *Subliminal* 82). When we are not Gathering effectively, we do not know the real emotions or buttons to push to capture and inspire a limbic response—steering someone's elephant. Story Telling alone can be interesting, but not effective. The magic of Gathering is the personal and emotional context that allows you to tailor a specific and inspiring story. Human attention is a scarce resource today. You will be memorable Gathering another person's story, and astounded by the affect it will have on him.

Have you ever heard the old story about the Hawthorne plant called the "Hawthorne Effect?" It is the story of a new plant manager who, in trying to improve workers' productivity, decides to turn the lights up. Productivity miraculously improves, but the manager guesses wrong on why. After surveying the employees, he finds out they are working harder because they now think the new manager *cares* more about them, not just because the lighting improved. Didn't he turn up the lights to make them more comfortable while they worked? These people felt like someone finally paid attention to their needs, which in turn, shifted their internal story about management, changed their feelings, and led to action.

Later, we will tell you a story about Colonel Joshua Chamberlain during the U.S. Civil War, but we also want to mention a few things about him now. He gave a very moving story to 120 Maine deserters. Before he crafted this story, he realized that the soldiers were thirsty from their long march and ordered a full mess for them. Then Colonel Chamberlain took the time to Gather their story and feel their emotions. He was trying to identify with them as Maine volunteers who had seen a lot of combat. He reflected back their story and promised to solve their enlistment problem after the battle. You will learn later of the great success of that story, but was it the Gathering that did it? Was it the Telling that did it? Or was it Gathering and caring, and then using that information to build an inspiring story? We believe that without the magical power of Gathering first, this story would not have been as effective. For this reason, we focus on and emphasize Gathering as a much more important and fundamental tool than Telling.

Mark Goulston tells the story of a very successful hostage negotiator. In this negotiation, a man is sitting in his car, attempting to commit suicide by holding a gun to his throat. The negotiator wants to help him by really understanding his story. He says, "I'll bet you feel that nobody knows what it's like to have tried everything else and be stuck with this as your only way out, isn't that true" (6)? The negotiator is then silent and patient, and most often, what follows a question like this is that people start to share their stories. The negotiator doesn't judge them, he doesn't get angry, and he certainly doesn't start negotiating right away. Instead, he responds to what they tell him with, "That must make you feel _____."

In the majority of situations where the negotiator can feel and play back the real emotions of the person he is trying to help, the situation ends well, like this one did. Not easily, not without some drama or negotiation, but without anyone getting killed. Unfortunately, empathic listening and playing back emotions is a rare skill. It is practiced and celebrated when it works by these types of professionals. Goulston calls the emotional response the negotiator elicits, "feeling felt"(45-54), and he says it is one of the most powerful emotions. When you truly believe that someone really knows how you feel, you identify, you feel safe, and you let your guard down. That is what happens in support groups. People tend to feel safe with other people who have felt their pain as they have experienced it and feel comfortable sharing both the facts and the emotions. But is it possible to feel it by Gathering their story?

Maya Angelou, a renowned poet and author who made a huge contribution to bettering the human condition, stated, "People will forget what you said, people will forget what you did, but people will never forget how you made them feel." Early in my career, I worked for a company called Management Science America (MSA). The founder and chairman was John P. Imlay[1]. He was a remarkable leader and public speaker, but he did not have a great memory for names, so he called almost everyone "Tiger." However, when you came in

---

1 Unfortunately, John Imlay passed away on March 22, 2015. He will be remembered fondly and with gratitude by the thousands of people he touched.

contact with him, he listened so carefully and thoughtfully that he made you feel like you were the most important person in the room. You just wanted to be a better person because of it. MSA was a great company in its day, but its lasting legacy is the number of wonderful leaders who were hired and groomed there, and who then moved on to lead, grow, and groom others. This intent focus by someone else can make you feel like you can be more than you think you can, and accomplish almost anything.

So if Gathering is so powerful and magical, how do we do it? The slow down part has to kick in because we are on a major dirt road here with a lot of potholes and other dangerous stuff. You really have to know your Why and want to acquire this skill and practice it until you can do it in the *flow*. It is simple, but not easy.

Why Is Story Gathering So Hard?

In a recent survey of Business to Business (B2B) salespeople, the best data available shows that only 2 percent have had formal listening training. And even if we have had training on listening, a lot of things going on in our brains work against our applying it. First of all, our subconscious brain is moving much faster than our conscious brain, so instead of actively listening, we are processing things we want to get done. And guess what? Humans express this processing in language. That is the powerful elephant sending this poor little rider signals to talk, and so what do you think happens? Most of us only have the ability to stay quiet for a short period of time.

In Gary Chapman's book, *The 5 Love Languages*, he cites a study that concluded that the average listening time before speaking is seventeen seconds. So how do we actively listen to someone telling a twenty-minute story about her great aunt, Gertrude, who is sick and ended up falling in the bathtub, and how they had to call the police to go get her? Then she had to drive three hours to get there, and upon arriving, had to listen to Uncle Bill talk about all of his problems? Now your elephant is raring: Get me out of here. Stop this dribble. Say something so she will be quiet. The reality of us not being able to listen for very long, coupled with the fact that people tend to tell long, drawn-out, and uninteresting stories, has continued to pave our superhighway of being active Tellers but lousy Gatherers.

What next exacerbates our poor Gathering ability is we have all been taught that smart people ask a lot of questions. In sales, we call this selling method "diagnose and prescribe," and Neil Rackham, the father of modern sales training, Spin Selling, taught it to everyone. In ancient Greece, they called it the Socratic method of questioning to find answers. In the medical, psychological, and social work fields, professionals have been taught this questioning methodology as well. The problem is that this technique derails our story by interrupting the Teller and badgering him with questions. It causes the Teller to become frustrated by taking him off point, and thereby, not letting his natural story unfold or gain true understanding. Worse yet, people definitely do not "feel felt," and they quite often become annoyed.

Again, think about your brain as a submerged iceberg. Besides the neural connections, highways, and dirt roads, two personae are lurking underneath. One is more effective, a curious detective, and the other is an obnoxious defense attorney.

J. Dickinson

Figure 2.1

Figure 2.1

They both ask questions and come to conclusions in exactly the same way, yet each uses an entirely different process. The detective observes his surroundings. He tries to get a real feel for the crime scene. He tries to let one piece of data lead him to another, and although possibly forming some hypotheses, he is always cross-checking and finding real facts to substantiate or invalidate. Great detectives stay curious longer, double-check more often, and listen very carefully and empathically. Often, when they do this well and are patient, the stars align, bringing the truth to light.

The defense attorney doesn't want to observe much or even know all of the data. He wants to listen quickly to his client, glossing over most of the real details and not digging very hard or cross-checking much. He then comes to some conclusion or *spin* that could possibly get the guilty person off—his defense story. He then only gathers data that matches his hypothesis and rejects everything else that might get in the way: murder weapon, eyewitness accounts, blood on clothes.... None of that stuff deters our defense attorney and his elephant, which just plods along with his side of the story. Now the nasty part is that when the attorney gets the prosecution's witnesses on the stand, he badgers them, firing question after question until sometimes they just can't think straight. He tries to take them off their own story and push them into directions they did not want to go. Flustered, upset, and pressed, many times, they just shut down. Haven't you seen that episode?

Now, we all are probably thinking, *Who acts like this guy?* Well, I have often, Christine, sometimes, and possibly even some of you. Think about it. Have you ever interrupted someone with a question before he or she was finished speaking? Was your brain ever racing to the next question you would ask or thinking about how you were going to respond before the other person had her whole thought or story out? If you have not, then you are a pretty amazing rider, and we salute you. However, for most of us, the seventeen-seconds-of-silence rule holds true; we diagnose and prescribe, and we allow that darn defense attorney to interrupt and start asking questions. Is that effective? Does it make the other person feel heard? Does it even allow her to get out the real story?

Christine invented an effective exercise that we use in our workshops to demonstrate that people have been trained to act more like defense attorneys than curious detectives. She gives a brief description about a situation, and then she asks the audience to find out what happened. For the most part, their defense attorneys take over. Instead of letting the story naturally unfold, participants begin to pepper Christine with questions. They lead with questions to uncover the story they *think* is happening and have already told themselves, and therefore, they uncover a lot of useless things that have nothing to do with the point; the *why* of the real story. However, the defense attorneys know that these facts are important because they will lead to their preconceived notion of the story.

I would love to divulge the actual story Christine uses, but I need to create some curiosity about our workshops. Suffice it to say, in all of the times doing this exercise, not one group has gotten to the real story Christine wanted to tell. Oh, they found out a lot of interesting information that they did not know. They let the defense attorney go unchecked, jumping to conclusions, and questioning till the bitter end. Some felt they were good attorneys, but they never got the accurate story; they certainly lost the case with Christine. Furthermore, they lost the case without even realizing it, in very short order, I might add. In sales workshops, we discuss this as one of the traits of "Impatient Selling"— asking so many questions that people feel badgered and not at all enthusiastic about answering them. "Asking lots of questions is a good way to destroy someone's story—not to mention break the flow of introspection the storytelling might have begun"(Simmons 194).

Most of the time, our questions validate the defense we already have made, and even though these assumptions are often wrong, we are still driven to find the story we know is right, even when it's not. Why do our defense attorneys do this? Why do smart people make dumb mistakes? Why is it so hard to Gather stories by letting them unfold naturally? Is there another way to Gather the real story, acting more like our curious detective? The answer is a definitive yes!

Gathering Stories Can Create Magic

We believe that Story Gathering opens up the potential for more magic. It is a simple process, although not easy, as evidenced by the potholes on the dirt road called Empathic Listening. Annette Simmons, in her book *The Story Factor*, mentions an interesting moment during one of her talks on genuine listening versus behavioral listening. One of the female participants bluntly grabbed the group's attention by stating: "Listening is just like sex. If the desire is there, the skills will follow" (183). Now, we are not sure what to think about that story, but Christine and I at least agree with the last part about becoming good at listening. We can all get better at it—and possibly even good at it. If you really want to get the story, you will become curious and patient enough like the detective to make that connection and find it. I know, who has time for making human connections in this harried world? Did we not just get a text we have to respond to?

However, listening patiently and staying curious is hard. We already mentioned the bit about us not being able to listen too long to something (the seventeen-seconds statistic). Well, there is also another reason that makes listening difficult; that is, most Tellers are not very good at Telling their stories. As storytellers, we go off on tangents—our brain thinks of something relatable to what we are saying, but not relevant to the story, and we say it anyway. We haven't really prepared the story, so it may not have the right flow, and we may be jumping from place to place. Imagine a confusing story being told to impatient listeners who want to ask a lot of questions that may not really enhance or uncover the real story. Been there, done that.

Now, imagine if we slowed down, and in the end, got there faster. What if we heard the whole story? What if we asked some open-ended questions that got the Teller to be more concise in the telling, while we just listened really hard and observed? What if we took the Teller back to the beginning, truly understanding all of the relevant parts to the story: The Background, Struggles, Tipping Point, and New Beginning? Maybe something fantastic would happen, like his true feelings or the real *why* would emerge, and we would understand enough to be more relevant and effective as we related our next story to him.

Christine was fortunate enough to have had this formal training. When she understood the client's story—the facts, emotions, and the *why*—it was called "listening with the third ear." In our workshops, we ask participants to go home and tell a short story of something that happened: when they made a mistake, were vulnerable, and recovered. Next, the person should look at his kids, partner, or friend and say, "Tell me about your day." Then listen for as long as the Teller talks. Yes, JUST LISTEN. We've heard some amazing stories resulting from this simple act. Maybe it's about a teenage boy who never talks at the dinner table, but this time, opens up because his dad told him a story. Now the teen is interacting with his parents, truly having fun, instead of hurrying back to texting.

Recently, Jane, a workshop participant, told us a story about trying this exercise with a friend on the phone. First, Jane told a quick story; then she asked her friend, "What about you?" The more actively Jane listened, the more intense the conversation became. After seven minutes of uninterrupted listening, with Jane just being present, her friend burst into tears and told a very personal and emotional story. Jane was stunned by the feeling and vulnerability her friend relayed. She had no idea that any of it was taking place in her friend's life. At that moment, Jane realized the magic of Gathering, of letting a story unfold naturally, and really understanding the other person's feelings. She experienced the effect of letting her friend, "feel felt," and she grasped how genuine and powerful this tool could be to have a meaningful and satisfying conversation. Story Gathering helped Jane's friend move from the stuck place she had been, to another, more positive place, open to taking a Nudge in the right direction.

What is happening here? Is this good or bad? Do we really want to understand people this way in the business world? Our research and practice tell us that we do because it will definitely help us connect better with others, understanding their stories, potholes and all, and possibly helping people with a new story that will lead to a Nudge in a different direction. Hey, we understand how nice this stateroom has been, but very soon it will fill up with water and become dangerous. How about heading toward the lifeboats to return to safety with our families?

To be an effective Story Teller, we need to learn how to Gather first. Everyone knows that Abraham Lincoln was a famous storyteller, and that he used this tool as he barnstormed for votes and led his difficult cabinet. What Pulitzer-Prize-winning historian Doris Kearns

Goodwin unveils in her book *Team of Rivals* is that Lincoln spent many hours as a young boy around the campfire, listening to the stories of trappers, traders, and adventurers. During this time, Lincoln's father owned a trading post which was on the crossroads to the West, and he always kept a fire going to bring together these travelers and hear the exciting and emotional stories of their journeys and adventures. "Young Abe listened so intently to these stories, crafted from experiences of everyday life, that the words became embedded in his memory" (50). These early years were formative for Lincoln. They taught him effectively to Gather Stories and then deliver them with the correct word pictures and emotions to make his points stick, causing people to take Action.

Chapter Reflections

1. Certain tools can help us better understand people so we can help them unleash their potential.

   - TATN Framework is the car.

   - Personality Profiles are the tires

   - Story (Gathering and Building/Telling) is the engine

   - Nudges are the gas pedal

2. Personality profiles provide insight into people's natural tendencies and their ability to adapt and be flexible. A profile is useful in learning about ourselves and others to align and fast-track our communication for action and results.

3. The use of Story:

   • Storytelling is one of the most natural things humans have been doing for over 95,000 years. It engages the limbic brain, which is where our stories reside. We recommend six story categories: Vision Stories, Strategy Stories, Culture Stories, Company Stories, Customer Stories, Why I Do What I Do Stories, and Lessons Learned Stories.

   • Effective leaders throughout the ages have used stories to inform, educate, convince, and inspire (Jesus, Lincoln, and Martin Luther King Jr., for example).

   • We record information in stories and actually understand our history and motivations through story, shaping our current feelings and actions. Story Gathering is not as natural, and it can create magic because humans have a deep-rooted need to be understood. Few of us take the time in our harried world to learn and practice effective Gathering (Defense Attorney vs. Curious Detective). Story Gathering is a more critical skill than Story Telling.

Nudges

1. Take or review your Personality Profile to gain insight about yourself and how to adapt to other styles.
2. Reflect on a story that was told to you that impacted your life by changing the course of your actions.
3. In the next few days, be consciously aware how often someone is Telling a story or taking the time to Gather a story: at work, home, or with friends. How many of these stories made a clear point, and how often do people Tell vs. Gather a story?

Chapter 3
TATN Steps 1 & 2: Know What You Want and WHY; Understand The Stories Being Told

Christine has many stories from her work with her mentor, Andy, where, after multiple discussions with their clients, it became apparent that the clients really did not know what they were doing or why. People were so conditioned to travel mindlessly down their superhighways that they did not even realize the effects or implications of those actions. This situation reminds us of the story about a lady who was cooking a ham. Before she put it in the pan, she cut one quarter of the ham off, and then put it in the oven. Her husband, being an accomplished cook himself, was puzzled by this action, and asked, "Why do you cut a quarter of the ham off before putting it in the pan?" His wife was startled by the question, but on reflection, she said, "I really don't know, but that's the way my mom always did it." Being a curious detective, the husband called his mother-in-law, who gave him the same reply. Fortunately, the grandmother was still alive, vibrant, and feisty, and when he posed the same question to her, he got a different response entirely. "That's simple," she told him. "The pan I used to cook the ham was too small, so I had to cut a little bit off to get the ham to fit."

How many other situations can you recall in your personal and professional lives where you mindlessly followed a paved superhighway without taking the time to ask "Why?" and understand the current story? We think if you reflect for just a bit on this question, you will find you have experienced more of these situations than you initially thought, and many of those superhighways do not really help us unleash our potential.

Knowing What You Want and Why

To unleash potential, we believe it is critical for our communication framework to first start with the reason: Know what you want and why. If we remember back to the story of *Alice in Wonderland*, we learned that as long as we did not know where we were going, any road would take us there. Whether you are taking out the trash or planning your newest mobile app that will revolutionize the world, you have to start with "Know what you want and why."

If you cannot answer this question first, you should put it on the backburner like a teakettle and come back to it later. As a matter of fact, we strongly recommend not to tackle any of the other steps until this first step is really clear in your mind—that you actually can articulate what you want and why, and that you believe the *why* is powerful enough to sustain you on the dirt road as you hit potholes. Getting too far out in front of your supply lines in combat, as Napoleon learned while attacking Russia, or taking too many actions without knowing where you are going, might just result in something happening that you do not want: a little less ham. Authors call this foundational insight many things: purpose, vision, mission, big ideas, goals, etc. Stephen Covey's third habit in his book *The 7 Habits of Highly Effective People* is to "put first things first." Douglas Smith in *Happiness* calls it "purpose," and says it "is like underwear; don't be caught without it" (118)! General David Petraeus talks about getting the "big ideas" right. Christine and I call it "Know what you want and why."

Simon Sinek, author of the book, *Start with Why,* gives a brilliant TED Talk called "How Great Leaders Inspire

Action." His ideas have been influential in formulating our beliefs on the importance of knowing your *why*. If you watch his TED Talk video, you'll further realize the importance of taking this first step in TATN. I mean, don't all of us say that we will do or that we want to do things that we end up not doing? And what's really driving us? If you want to make a lot of money, is it really the money you are after, or is it something else? Is it the satisfaction or prestige, is it competing to be at the top of your game, or is it the pleasure of serving your customers? If you want to be a nurse, is it because you want to take blood, deal with sick people, and work all night, or is it because you have a deep sense of service, and want to spend your life giving back to others? Do you know the real *what* and *why*?

We believe that without a powerful *why* or belief, you may just have a temporary *what* that will either get forgotten after some time, or not withstand the jarring of all of the potholes on that dirt road. You certainly will not persist long enough to begin executing in the *flow*. There's a story about three Italian construction workers in Brooklyn after World War II. A man walks by as they are working on a building and observes something puzzling. The first two workers look somewhat interested, but a little sloppy in their work. However, the third guy stands out. Since the man walking by has a minute and is curious about what could be so apparently different in their actions, he simply asks them, "What are you doing?" The first guy says, "Laying bricks," the second guy says, "Building this building," but the third guy looks up with a big smile and proudly says, "I am helping to build this church where my friends and family can come to gather and worship our God." Did this man's strong belief inspire his actions in any way? Was his performance better because he had a why, and not just a what? Did his actions and joy while working increase his performance compared to the other workers? Was he truly working in the flow? We think so.

The tools of personality profile and story can help you here. If you have taken a personality profile, it is worth looking at it again to understand your core personality as you attempt to uncover your true *what* and *why*. Are you fast-paced and outspoken or cautious and reflective? Are you accepting and warm or questioning and skeptical? How do you make decisions? How do you change decisions? How does what you need to do or are doing tap into the core strengths of your personality? Do you have to use a lot of energy to flex? How important is the what/why you are struggling with, and how long do you need to let these questions percolate to find the real and true answers?

Truly understanding your personality can help you

reach important answers with some additional insight, and may just give you the little Nudge you need. Now couple this understanding with Gathering your current story. Why are you here trying to decide this right now? What has brought you to this point? Why are you doing this? What do you really want to accomplish? Are you doing this just because it is superhighway habit? Is it a Decisive Action that will help you achieve something meaningful? Can you uncover the current story being told and reflect it back verbally or write it down to help you come to a better answer?

We have observed many people struggle with these questions, but these two tools (personality profiles and story) can help. We know there is not only one right way, but we have seen the additional insight that can come if you slow down and really get these answers. It will truly help you speed up. We are also very convinced that if you are not curious or patient enough to complete this important first step and just rush to the other steps, you may not realize the full potential. Many people find themselves stuck, failing to execute, or circling back because they have skipped this first step.

Christine has a story about an HVAC company she works with called Tozour Energy Systems that emphasizes this idea of really knowing the *why* in Step 1 of TATN.

All of the customer service reps were women in a male-dominated industry. Frank, the Executive VP, had me working with the reps on their professional development. I found out that they all loved their jobs, and what's more, they really had a passion for what they were doing—a level of commitment and genuine excitement to come to work each day. Frankly, the more time I spent with these women, the more puzzled I became over the enthusiasm for their work. Why were these dynamic women so jazzed about working in the HVAC field? I mean, some days they were climbing on rooftops or talking about service contracts for things like chillers. I knew that Tozour was a great place to work, but that wasn't enough for me to reconcile the love for their job as opposed to just loving where they worked.

One day, as I was conducting coaching assessment meetings, my curiosity took over, so I asked each of the reps separately, "Help me understand something here; I really don't get it. Why do you love working in the HVAC field?" Katie was the first person I asked, and she responded, with a big smile on her face, "I really like helping people." I said to Katie, "Really? Well, how are you helping people?" Katie went on to say, "Are you kidding? What could deliver a better service to a company than to make sure people are working in a comfortable environment, cool enough in the summer and warm enough in the winter? We relieve our customers' stress by helping them navigate crises when something isn't working. Furthermore, when we get our customers to commit to a service contract, we partner with them to make sure these emergencies are tempered, all with the end goal of maximizing the comfort and productivity of their employees."

To my amazement, each rep I talked with that day had almost the exact same answer as Katie. Suddenly, it dawned on me: If these answers were such an unexpected surprise to me, I wondered what their managers thought got these women up in the morning and excited about coming to work. So I scheduled a meeting with the four managers (all male, by the way) and asked them just that. Here are some of the responses I got: "Oh, they like the bonuses they get for meeting their goals," or "They like having control over the amount of money they can earn," etc., etc., all external rewards. When I told them their answers weren't even close, that their customer services reps liked helping people, I could see their collective mouths drop. I said, "Look, guys; if you don't tap into this core motivation, you are missing the boat to motivate and help these women grow your business." That day at Tozour, I was again reminded of the power of truly understanding other people's whys and helping senior and middle management understand the power of it, too.

Upon discussing the customer services reps' shared why, Frank implemented some Nudges in their hiring process. Although Tozour had already done this intuitively in hiring, management added specific interview questions to ensure that all hires had this same strong why. Frank took the lessons learned about the reps from getting their why, and used it in a critical sales meeting with a potentially big prospect to drive outcomes. Rather than having the reps just say their name, their role, and how long they worked for the company (you know, all the usual stuff we say at these meetings), Frank had the reps simply say their name and why they do what they do in thirty seconds. The feedback at that meeting from the prospect was that it was the best introductory meeting they ever had because they felt they really knew the people from whom they were buying. Tozour ultimately won the business, and Frank attributes this to the small Nudge and new approach.

As you can see, small Nudges yielded some dramatic results for the company simply because Christine and Frank slowed down to truly understand the why of the people doing the work. Once the reps' belief was identified and specific, it could be harnessed to tap more potential. You may be surprised by some of the whys that people you are in contact with have, and how you can use them to inspire Nudges for higher performance. All this being said, please spend as much time as needed on the Know What You Want and Why step of TATN to determine what you want and even more importantly, *why* you want it. What strong belief of yours does a certain activity satisfy? Does it fuel your passions? Does it cause you to give your very best and continue to strive to improve? Or is it just a "Ho-Hum Why" that tells you to do it quickly and be done with it.

Knowing the *what* and *why* is certainly critical for big decisions in life, like whom to marry, what career path to take, what kind of company to start, or when to transition out. However, if you know these whats and whys clearly, they will also guide you through all of the little decisions and choices you have to make daily, as you are bombarded by information in this fast-paced world: what meeting to go to, what customer to go see, what sales rep to work with, or what project to focus on first. By answering these questions and making choices with your whys in mind, you will do more of the important things and tap into your passions. When you do this more effectively, you will leverage your strengths and have more *flow* moments. If you remember from our brain science superhighways, these Whys will be powerful enough to help you build new highways from dirt roads, and not just turn back to the old tried and true. An old mentor of John's, founder of The Complex Sale, Rick Page, used to ask a very important question: "What would I die for?" He believed that if he knew what he would die for, he would better know how to live each day, prioritizing his actions to become more effective.

Understand the Current Story: "Gathering"

Okay, so once you know what you or others want and why, you have to understand the current story being told that is influencing your existing feelings and actions. As a useful metaphor, think of your situation as a play, movie, or drama. Identify the characters, their roles, and struggles. Remember that in your powerfully fast subconscious brain, a story is being crafted and told. Here is a quick story that makes this point.

A lawyer in New York City had a particularly horrible

week. He was looking forward to his weekend: a quiet evening, a relaxing Saturday, and a calm and meditative service at St. Patrick's Cathedral early Sunday morning. Everything was going as planned until he got on the F train. He sat across from a man with five young children who were bouncing around, making loud noises, and being extremely disruptive. At first, the lawyer attempted to ignore the shenanigans, but he couldn't stop his fast subconscious brain (elephant) from building a story. It went something like, "What is wrong with this guy? He needs to get control of his kids. They need some discipline and a good talking to. What the hell?" After repeating this story in his conscious brain several times, he could no longer contain himself. Standing up aggressively, he yelled at the man. "What the heck is wrong with you? Are you deaf and blind? Don't you see how your kids are interrupting everyone else on this train? Get control of them NOW!" The man looked up, startled, but with a very sad face and tears in his eyes, replied, "I am so sorry. I haven't been paying any attention. You see, my wife just died this morning in the hospital from cancer, and I am overcome with grief. I really do apologize for my children's behavior." The lawyer was jolted with remorse, feeling awful and ashamed of his misunderstanding of the situation. At that moment, he would have done anything he could to console this man in mourning.

What a shift! Why was the lawyer no longer angry? How did he suddenly start thinking and acting with someone else's interests at heart? We believe, like current neuroscientists, that this immense shift in feeling and actions occurred when he heard the widower's story. Before hearing the real story, he was repeating his own story. It is pretty easy to understand and think that the lawyer was rational, right, and should have confronted the other man. But after hearing and processing a different story, the lawyer's feelings changed toward the situation. He definitely had a better understanding and greater empathy, and possibly would take a different action.

Now, we are not saying that it always happens like this, but we hope you can see how making a limbic connection and point with story can help you see something from a new perspective. And if you do, it might divert you from your wrong superhighway to the appropriate dirt road, pretty easily sometimes. We also know that unless you truly understand the story you are telling yourself or understand the stories others are telling themselves, you will not really know what is going on and how or what to Nudge. Remember the Event/(Story)/Feelings/Action Cycle that you now know has your subconscious brain telling you an immediate story? It is lurking under the tip of the iceberg and you may not really even be aware it, but rest assured, the story is being told. Does the F train story help you realize why it is so important to understand the current stories being told? You will have a strong ally in that information, which we will expound upon in later chapters to show you how it can help. But first, let's talk about how you Gather those stories.

Gathering Stories to Uncover the What and Why

Inside each of us are some very cool stories of who we are and why we do what we do. Usually we just never have the time or patience in listening really to understand it all. Why do we not know that our colleague, Joe, is a concert violinist? Or Sally, the lady in the next cubicle, was on the LPGA tour? Or that Don has donated his time to Big Brothers Big Sisters for eighteen years and mentored over fifty kids? More importantly, why don't we know *why* they really work here? This is one effect of the fast-paced digital society we live in. There is no time to slow down and have meaningful dialogue that creates connection unless we are very intentional about making time for this. Story Gathering is really the next thing we teach in our workshops after learning about the brain, our almost unlimited potential, and TATN. Story Gathering is where the real magic happens (and it is quite fun too, if you are curious). That is why, for us, it is much more important than just Telling Stories.

Christine once conducted a short seminar with a large, well-known private school in Philadelphia called Germantown Academy. Sue, a former client of Christine's, had just been appointed as the Lower School Head. Sue was taking the reins of the Lower School at a time when the teaching staff and team were feeling a great sense of disconnect, and they were fractured based on the leadership style of her predecessor. Sue knew that Germantown Academy had an excellent reputation and heritage. She also knew that times were shifting in the private school world, so maybe the school would need to try some different things to continue to serve the students, parents, and community even better by ultimately "meeting the children and parents where they are."

Sue is a very smart and astute executive, so she knew she would have to socialize this *why*—meeting them where they are—with the teachers and staff in order to be effective. She needed the staff to reconnect with each other and help each other buy into and embrace the vision for the upcoming school year. So Sue reached out to Christine for help in this task. They collaborated on how they could help the teachers reconnect, by uncovering their whats and whys. Sue and Christine conducted a large meeting with the teachers, asking one teacher (the designated listener) to gather a colleague's story, while the large group of teachers all watched and listened quietly.

The listener was to gather: 1) Why the teacher had come to Germantown Academy, 2) What he or she wanted to accomplish, and most importantly, 3) Why he or she became a teacher in the first place. Christine armed the listeners with 6 Gathering Questions™ (we will introduce these later) that were to be the only questions/statements they could use to Gather their colleagues' stories. This structure helped immensely.

Although it took a little time for some of the teachers to get to their what and why, remarkable things started happening when they told their stories. Walls of past distrust crumbled, feelings of mutual respect and pride became evident, and a new spirit of teamwork and collaboration emerged. Christine continues to work with Germantown Academy, and Sue believes that this watershed event using Story Gathering was a critical catalyst in making some fast-paced changes and harnessing the collective potential of the teaching team.

We believe Story Gathering is significant because it is where we learn the true struggles and the real implications on people and organizational performance; it is where we find out what is really going on. Story Gathering allows us to collect the visceral emotions that help us understand the person as we hear his or her story, and it provides an aperture into the underworld of the iceberg, limbic to limbic.

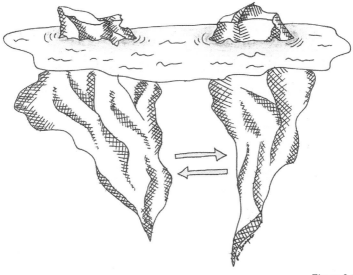

Figure 3.1

It is the tool that can help you make others "feel felt," and by doing so, help a person understand his or her own story better—what is holding the person back or what potential he or she may have. Real understanding will help form a bond that is very strong and show you how to build a story that will inspire others. Once you experience someone truly Gathering your story this way, or you Gather someone else's story this way, we guarantee that your relationship will never be the same. It will be infinitely more robust, honest, and real. "Really?" you ask.

One of the outcomes of the Germantown Academy Story Gathering session was a Nudge that Sue initiated and the teachers embraced: they posted their beliefs and whys on their classroom doors for all the students, teachers, and parents to see. The students and parents were both astonished and appreciative, thus creating a more meaningful bond.

As we discussed earlier, most of us do not really tell crisp, cohesive stories. So why would we think that we are effective Gatherers who can help uncover the true story? Well, what if you could? Would this make you more memorable and set you apart? Would you have the magic of the hostage negotiator and be able to understand people better? We think so. We have seen it in ourselves and in our customers, and we know that you can learn and apply this tool as well. However, there are some potholes.

What Gets in the Way of Story Gathering?

Before we jump into our Story Gathering MAP™, let's spend a few minutes talking about why it is difficult to Gather Stories. If we remember the brain science part, you know that a lot of stuff is going on under the iceberg with the elephant that can inhibit our listening ability. We learned that those 80 billion neurons fire and process fast. We know they send information to the rider quickly and in big bursts, much faster than the rider can handle his 3/5/7/9. We also know that those superhighways took a long time to build and have been well-traveled. If all this is happening, then it makes sense that when someone is talking, all those neurons are firing and will most likely send messages to the rider. If we are honest with ourselves, we know our elephant is constantly in motion, becoming impatient quickly and then interrupting with questions.

I must admit I constantly work on trying to be patient. My brain processes at a fast rate of speed and sets my mouth in gear as the defense attorney. Unfortunately, interrupting with questions is natural for some of us, and most of the time, it is not as helpful as we think. As mentioned earlier, according to Gary Chapman in *The 5 Love Languages*, the average individual listens for only seventeen seconds before interrupting and interjecting his own ideas. Chapman also states: "If I give you undivided attention while you are talking, I will refrain from defending myself or hurling accusations at you or dogmatically stating my position. My goal is to discover your thoughts and feelings. My objective is not to defend myself or set you straight. It is to understand you" (64). So, remember, slow down and Gather the full story—facts and emotions. We need to teach your rider to harness the elephant and the fast quantum brain.

Another major challenge to Story Gathering has been drilled into most of us—we have been taught problem solving, or as they say in the sales world, how to "diagnose and prescribe." Of course, fundamental to diagnosing is asking really good questions, and if you are like me, you have been through Solution Selling and Spin Selling. Remember 9 Boxes, 400 Questions, and make that person answer, darn it! How else can you really get someone's information if you don't ask him a ton of questions, leading him to where you think he should go? This all makes good sense; unfortunately, it just does not work most of the time, and like some other ideas, turns out to be faulty. Remember the "Earth is flat" and the "geocentric model of the world?"

Luckily, Christine was not trained with this in vogue "diagnose and prescribe" method during her psychological services training. She learned that you have to connect with someone first before you "earn the right" to ask any questions. Psychologists call this "joining," and if the joining does not occur, you have to stay patient until it does. As it turns out, this was very insightful training. What we know now, with the new developments in brain science, is that Christine's training was spot on. We have to connect with people at the limbic, submerged, elephant level. When we ask someone a lot of questions, we take him back to the rider, the conscious, 3/5/7/9, logical brain. So, in effect, instead of making a limbic connection and hearing someone's real story, we are hearing another one, forced by us. Furthermore, if we start the questions too early, we begin taking people in a direction they really did not want to go. We both end up meandering down this path, not realizing that we are not getting and they are not telling the real story.

Okay, so most people cannot tell well-crafted, coherent stories, and you want to help them. Early on, you begin asking questions that you are thinking about—questions that interest you. These questions may take the Teller in a different direction from the story she is trying to tell or wants to tell. The questions may not have any bearing on the real story and worse yet, put both of you in your rational, logical brains.

I recently met with a partner who was very well-trained in the "diagnose and prescribe" methodology. Jay started the conversation by asking me a question. Instead of deflecting it and trying to determine what we both wanted to talk about and why, I launched off into a detailed answer to his question. Well, Jay, in the moment, became a great defense attorney, so he formulated another question and fired it at me before he fully heard my response to the first. The second question took me in a different direction, and in the middle of attempting to answer it, the defense attorney launched yet another question that he wanted answered. Of course, at this point, we were heading down the path to nowhere. Two past questions were dangling in the air unfinished.

After twenty minutes of frustration and very little true dialogue or understanding, Jay said, "Gee, you won't answer any of my questions." I almost fired back, "Hold on. You keep peppering me with the next question before I can get through the first." As you can imagine, this meeting did not go favorably for either one of us. Jay was extremely frustrated that I would not answer his questions to get where he wanted to take me. I was frustrated because I could never really tell my true story.

This anecdote is instructive because it happens more often than we realize. We definitely see it every day on TV, as pundits badger each other with questions, while no one is really Gathering the story. Often the scenario breaks down into two or more people talking over each other to try to make their points because both have stopped listening. How often does this scene play out in your world? How often do you feel frustrated when it happens to you? And maybe worse, how often do you become the defense attorney, questioning and creating feelings of frustration in others? Well, as a Mars guy, I am used to doing this more often than I would like to admit. However, by actively using our 6 Gathering Questions™ and Story Gathering tool, I am getting better.

Statistics show that a vast majority of salespeople who have been trained on "diagnose and prescribe" methodologies are not successful with them. When we have not connected with people at the limbic level, and not earned the right to ask questions, they will recoil and clam up when we pepper their conscious brains. Have you ever been grilled by someone, and interrupted in the middle of your thoughts with questions? Does this make you feel defensive and confused, taking you off of your main train of thought? How do you get back to your natural story? I am sure we can all identify with this situation and the disconnection and frustration it causes. So why do we use this approach on others whom we are trying to connect with and understand?

Now, Christine and I are not exactly sure how these "diagnose and prescribe" methodologies came about, but we do know that fMRI technology did not exist when the methodologies were formulated, and yet they continue to be taught and espoused today as a sure-fire method. These questions and interruptions can be really frustrating because they can destroy someone's story. Story Gathering is a more effective skill and can augment what you've already learned.

We believe our Story Gathering MAP™ will really help you here. Let us tell you how.

Our Story Gathering MAP™

We have developed a Story Gathering MAP™ (S.G.M.) with 6 Gathering Questions™ that will help you pivot from diagnose and prescribe to Gathering, allowing the story to unfold naturally. You can use some or all of these questions to help you fill out each section of the Story Gathering MAP™. (Please refer to page 137 for an illustration of our Story Gathering MAP™).

Please be sure to gather all the information in each block of the MAP before moving on to the next one. You will find in doing this that using the question, "Before we move ahead, can you tell me more?" works wonders. The key to each block of the MAP is getting both the facts and the emotions, and helping the Teller slow down to recount his or her whole story.

Here's an outline for the Story Gathering MAP™:

1. What is the Background/Beginning? Who are the characters and what are their roles?

2. What is the Middle/Struggles? What is the impact and whom does it affect? Why?

3. What is the Tipping Point/Critical Event? Is it explicit or hidden? Who cares?

4. What is the Ending/New Beginning?

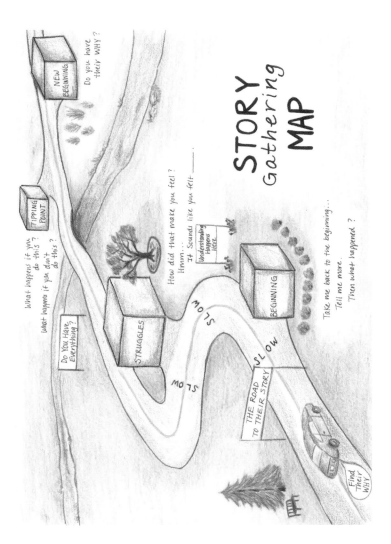

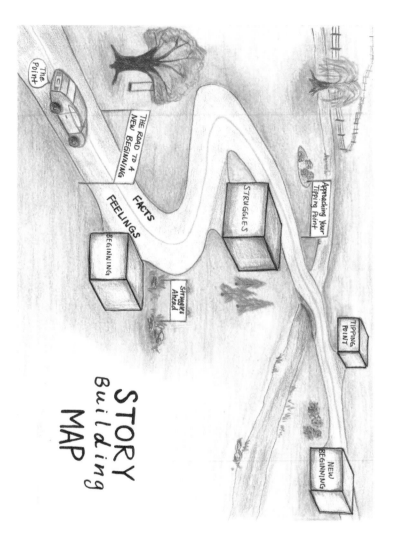

When we first suggest this method to people, it feels counterintuitive. We observe more defense attorneys than curious detectives. Why would seasoned professionals need 6 Gathering Questions™ and a Story Gathering MAP™? Well, what we do know is that these tools just plain work, helping you get the real story. And if these tools even have the remote possibility of helping people to master this skill, why not try it and see what happens? We predict a "Wow."

We have seen firsthand that people who use this tool and these questions just inherently become better listeners and more in touch with the emotional context of the conversation. We do not have to teach them a complicated listening model or lecture them on Emotional Intelligence. We just have to ask them to try this process and practice it so that it becomes subconscious and natural. Yes, like Annette Simmons' workshop participant inferred, if you want to learn how to do it, you can.

We do ask you to put your obnoxious defense attorney away. If you already know the story and want to pepper the witness with questions to elicit your version, you will never be curious enough to understand the real story. So please just hold that dude down for a bit and, instead, bring out your curious detective. Observe what is going on. Look around. Get a feel for the crime scene. Give your full attention to the person who knows the story. Just breathe and listen. No talking. No peppering. Just pretend you are in a new movie and do not know what you do not know.

Help the Teller fully develop the Background/Beginning. Discover his Struggles and how they affect the key people—and make sure you let the Teller fully develop this section before moving on. Remember, the struggles are the most interesting part anyway. Then find the Tipping Point. Do you really understand the emotions that the person is feeling as he tells his story? What are they? Be totally engaged, as if this is the most important information of your life, and that really bad things will happen if you don't get it. This person is the most important person in the world to you right now, and he is telling a captivating story and possibly sharing vulnerabilities that you have to Gather before going to the next step.

All right, you are relaxed. You're breathing calmly. You are so focused on the other person that your own elephant cannot even transmit any messages. So how do you maintain that presence and keep the elephant from turning into the defense attorney again as you listen fully and let the story unfold naturally? We have developed six questions/requests to help you achieve this goal. The trick is that these are the only questions and requests you can use.

The 6 Gathering Questions™:

1. Take me back to the beginning.
2. Tell me more.
3. Then what happened?
4. How did that make you feel?
5. Hmm...
6. It sounds like you felt _____?

Our usage of these open-ended Gathering Questions versus the defensive attorney's leading and badgering ones is almost therapeutic. The other person's limbic brain sees you engaged, which fires his neurons, fueling feelings of safety. You completely disarm the person when he hears you patiently asking him to go back to the beginning. Your intent listening and additional questions—"Then what happened? Tell me more. How did that make you feel?"—relax the automatic response of the elephant, allowing the elephant and rider to listen calmly to the whole story. The person then brings up the beginning of the story. If he isn't crisp in telling it, you nudge him, instead of jerking on the reins. Most people can deal with "Then what happened?" However, the "Hmm..." statement is a killer. Everyone in our workshops laughs hysterically when we introduce it. And then they try it. Oh, they will still laugh, but eventually, they are laughing at how quickly they rejected a question that turned out to be so powerful. When someone says, "Hmm" authentically, the limbic to limbic message is: "I am listening. I really am interested. I really care about you and your story."

Now, it is probably inappropriate to write this, but Christine can be mischievous from time to time. Sometimes, depending on the makeup of the group and appropriateness, she will state: "I can see some of you Mars People not believing this. Well, I will make you a little wager. Will you go home tonight and attempt to do this authentically with your spouse? It will not work if you are being funny and a smartass, but if you really try it with just these questions, and you are genuinely curious, and you really listen for a lot longer than your normal seventeen seconds, I predict that the evening might end very well indeed."

If you are from Venus, we know you know this will have an amazing result—although we do worry about sudden shocks to the poor woman whose husband suddenly became patient, attentive, and caring, at least for a short time. If you are a tough guy from Mars and really try it yourself, we are confident in the result and know you will be so delighted that you tried it. You will thank us and tell everyone you know about this cool book, so we decided to put it in. However, please do not attempt this exercise on your own tonight—only try it after appropriate training, or we cannot guarantee any outcomes.

By the way, we definitely cannot print the stories that are told the next day. Whew!! You would not believe how good of a Story Gatherer some of these guys become, literally overnight. We can guarantee that you would like to hear some of them...well, most of them—well, really all of them. Please feel free to ask Christine on a break during one of our workshops, and she will have you howling. By the way, this works for both men and women. There's just something magical here, especially when you reflect your partner's story back.

Reflecting Back Someone's Story Leads to "Genuine Understanding"

When you get good at Gathering someone's story, we believe it is important to reflect it back, for two reasons. The first is to show the other person that you were really listening and did get his or her story, facts, and emotions. The second is that, just in case you were not perfect (didn't we mention that already?), you will give the other person a chance to correct any misunderstandings. How many stories are currently being told that have glaring inaccuracies? Or worse yet, that you pretend are true because you have not done a really good job listening? We have found that these inaccurate stories often cause large problems for leaders and sales teams as they make decisions and take action based upon wrong assumptions. We help teams avoid these pitfalls, which is not that hard with some practice because all you have to do is repeat what you heard.

Let's take a few simple examples of reflecting back a story:

Example 1: Reflecting back from a well-known movie, *The Last of the Mohicans*:

Two Indians and a white man on the frontier have some harrowing adventures of trying to rescue two English maidens, with one girl and Indian dying in the process. Two lovers (the hero and one of the English maidens) and an old Indian are together at the end, but sad about their lost brethren. However, they are happy to live on in history.

Example 2: Personal reflection from one of our workshop participants:

"Gee, honey, I am really sorry. I now understand that you had a really bad day. The kids were late this morning and on your nerves all day. The washing machine broke down and nothing seemed to go right. You are feeling frustrated, angry, and agitated. You wish you could just have some quiet time to yourself. Why don't you go into the living room and lie on the couch, and I will get the kids to bed and give you time just to relax and decompress."

Example 3: Business reflection that helped close a deal:

Steve, a workshop participant, relayed the story of trying this process during a very tough, multi-million dollar negotiation. One of his VPs was negotiating a large contract and invited him on a sales call because they seemed stuck. Just by listening to the two negotiators with curiosity, he realized they were talking at each other and interrupting with neither understanding the real story. Steve was able to slow the situation down by asking the customer, Bill, to take him back to explain his position and why. After fully understanding, he was able to reflect the following: "Bill, it seems critical to your new corporate CIO to have this contract signed at a higher level than the division that is buying it. He wants this to concentrate risk at a higher level in your business and not burden the divisions. Do I get you? Because if that is accurate, we can certainly accommodate you. All we need to do is insert a clause that says that for this price, you only have the right to use the software for this division." Bill replied, "That is totally fine. This is not about price or use of the software; this is really about my new CIO's policy of how/where he wants to manage risk." Steve's VP was ecstatic. How did Steve do this? By slowing down, being curious, understanding the real story, and then reflecting it back.

We know that actively using our Story Gathering MAP™ will help in many situations, especially if you are directly working with people.

Chapter Reflections

1. Knowing the *what* and the *why* is the first place to start to tap into our potential and influence action. *Are you building a building or a cathedral?*

2. Many times we just jump into action and quit after hitting the first pothole. Without knowing our *why*, we will not be strong enough to sustain action. *Dirt Roads are unfamiliar and potentially dangerous.*

3. We all have an Inventory of Stories stored in our limbic brain that we tell to ourselves automatically. Listening (tuning in) to the stories we are telling ourselves gives us the insight to know whether these stories lead us to helpful or harmful actions in accomplishing our goals. *Event/(Story)/Feelings/ Action Cycle*

4. Gathering is not easy or as naturally intuitive as Telling. We are impatient and on average listen only seventeen seconds before we interrupt. Most people tell long rambling stories, which tries our patience further. We jump to conclusions quickly and ask questions that lead the "witness." *Defense Attorney*

5. A good story makes a clear point and captures the attention of the listener. Most good stories follow a natural progression, revealing both facts and emotions. *Story Gathering MAP™ (S.G.M.)*

6. Our 6 Gathering Questions™ help us slow down, leading the Teller back to the beginning. We become more curious and patient, letting the "real" story develop naturally, uncovering both the facts and the feelings of his or her story. *"Hmm…" and the Curious Detective*

7. Reflecting back is a tool to ensure that we have Gathered effectively. It is important to summarize, checkpoint, and re-gather if necessary. We can learn to do this well, and effective Gathering makes people feel important. *Maya Angelou: "I've learned that people will forget what you said, people will forget what you did, but people will never forget how you made them feel."*

Nudges

1. Reflect on a personal or business initiative that you have started and quit. What story were you telling yourself at the time? Did you know your *why*?

2. Think about "Why do I do what I do?" Then tell someone else this story. Is your *why* strong enough to sustain the actions you need to take to succeed?

3. Try to Gather someone else's story using our 6 Gathering Questions™. Think about how easy or hard this process was for you.

Chapter 4

TATN Steps 3 & 4:
Develop and Give Stories

Develop a New Story

So once you understand the stories being told, the third step is to develop a new story—one that is believable, emotional, and exciting. Christine and I have thought a lot about the story we are telling you and others. As we have shared, *our story* is the product of many things: research, practice, and experience with our clients, but the most important aspect may come from the discussions we have had about our own stories—the ones we have lived through separately, and the ones we have lived through together.

We often reflect back on that very tense day in the car that led to our "tipping point." Even though it was undoubtedly a very painful moment in our partnership, it was probably the most significant moment in the development of our story. I remember during one of our recent mind-melding sessions, Christine shared with me the story she was telling herself that day:

> You know John, I can still clearly remember the emotions I was experiencing…. As we headed out together in the morning, I felt very excited about our full day out with new prospects. I was convinced that the two of us together would be much more effective with our clients than either one of us could be alone.
>
> Looking back, I realize I took a lot for granted and assumed we would "just mesh" well on client calls. I mean, we had a plan, we had the balance of our experiences, and we believed the same things. However, as our day progressed and we met with clients, I began feeling pretty anxious and upset about how quickly you were moving. I tried to cue you to slow down, but to no avail.
>
> By the time we got in the car and I realized just how frustrated you were with me that I was

moving too slowly, I actually felt sick. You told me, "This is supposed to be fun, but I didn't have fun today." Those words rang in my ears—first, because I didn't want to contribute to you feeling anything less than good about working together, and second, because I wasn't having fun either.

I could sense the tension increasing between us because we weren't hearing one another; I was trying to be calm on the outside, even though I was anything but calm on the inside. When you said, "I'm not sure if this is going to work. Maybe we don't see the world the same way after all," I distinctly remember feeling relief in that moment, like, *Okay, maybe we don't, and I have a way out.* However, that sense of relief was fleeting and followed by an even sicker feeling at the thought of losing a partnership with you. I knew we had something special to offer together, but I was spinning and couldn't see in that moment how we could make it work.

After hearing Christine's response, I was thankful that we both agreed to take some time to consider what was best for each of us. To this day, I'm grateful that we came back together, realizing that we had hit the bottom of the pool and could push up for air together.

Fortunately, the strong personal bond we had formed over the last year and a half—sharing and working with clients and being very open with our beliefs, goals, and whys—kept us together.

I believe this incident pushed us to step back and ask ourselves some really important questions: What if we continued working together, combining our different approaches? What if our different approaches could be harnessed with an "and," not an "or"? And what if we could really help more people and organizations tap into their potential with these ideas? These thoughts caused new wirings and firings that helped us; they inspired us really to work and codify our ideas into a book and join our companies into CI Squared with a new focus.

Christine and I are still excited about the unlimited possibilities that the development of this new story helped us realize. It reminds us of another important story we mentioned earlier in this book: The story of Colonel Joshua Lawrence Chamberlain and the Maine Deserters from Michael Shaara's book *The Killer Angels*. This story portrays the key effect that our third step in the TATN Framework (Develop a New Story) can have on spurring others on to take action.

Colonel Chamberlain was put in charge of the Twentieth Maine Regiment in the Civil War at Gettysburg (by the way, if you have not read about him, he has a rather remarkable story as someone who impacted this country's history on the second day of the Gettysburg battle, winning the Congressional Medal of Honor). On this particular day, he was presented with 120 Maine deserters. These war-torn, weary men had been marching all day under guard and were hungry and thirsty. They particularly did not care for the foul-mouthed captain from the 118th Pennsylvania who had orders to turn them over to Colonel Chamberlain. The captain made it a point to emphasize that Chamberlain had the right to shoot them all if necessary.

However, Chamberlain, realizing the men were tired and hungry from the march and upset about the captain's mistreatment, immediately ordered his mess to get them well fed with plenty to drink. Then Chamberlain corralled the ring leader of the group to find out its story. The leader told him that these men had signed up voluntarily for two years of service. They had been in eleven battles with many wounded and a lot of friends killed, so they had seen firsthand the incompetence of the Union generals. It was the last straw when they found out that some paperwork glitch extended their two-year terms to three. So they just up and deserted because they were not going to fight anymore. What a tough position for Chamberlain. He knew the men's story was fairly accurate, so he wanted to let them go, but he needed them to fill his ranks for this important battle. He also certainly knew he would never shoot Maine soldiers who were most likely heroes.

So Colonel Joshua Chamberlain gathered the men around him and spoke from the heart:

> "Well, I don't want to preach to you. You know who we are and what we are doing here. But if you're going to fight alongside us there are a few things I want you to know. This Regiment was formed last fall, back in Maine. There were a thousand of us then. There's not three hundred of us now. But what is left is choice. Some of us volunteered to fight for the Union. Some came in mainly because we were bored at home and this looked like it might be fun. Some came because we were ashamed not to. Many of us came…because it was the right thing to do. All of us have seen men die. Most of us never saw a black man back home…. This is a different kind of army. If you look at history you'll see men fight for pay, or women, or some other kind of loot. They fight for land, or because a king makes them, or just because they like killing. But we're here for something new…. We're an army going out to set other men free…. This is free ground. All the way from here to the

Pacific Ocean. No man has to bow. No man born to royalty. Here we judge you by what *you* do, not by what your father was. Here you can be *something.* Here's a place to build a home. It isn't the land—there's always more land. It's the idea that we all have value, you and me, we're worth something more than the dirt. I never saw dirt I'd die for, and I'm not asking you to come join us and fight for dirt. What we're all fighting for in the end is each other."

Once he started talking he broke right through the embarrassment and there was suddenly no longer a barrier there. The words came out of him in a clear river, and he felt himself silent and suspended in the grove listening to himself speak...and he felt the power in him, the power of his cause. For an instant, he could see black castles in the air.... Then he was back in sunlit Pennsylvania. The bugles were blowing and he was done.... "I think if we lose this fight the war will be over. So if you choose to come with us I'll be personally grateful. Well. We have to move out." (M. Shaara 29-31)

In the end, 114 out of the original 120 joined with the Twentieth Maine and participated in one of the most famous battles of the Civil War: The Battle of Little Round Top. But why did they do it? They had already fought in many battles, been wounded, seen their friends killed, been led by lousy leaders, and they had already served their time. I think you all know the answer. Think back to Tony D'Amato's Inch by Inch story in *Any Given Sunday*, or William Wallace's story in *Braveheart*, or Marc Antony's story about Caesar, Cassius, and Brutus in Shakespeare's *Julius Caesar*.

Whether through some deep inspiration of the moment, with all the power of their conscious and subconscious brain, these rehearsed stories moved the masses. All of them are examples of developing a new story that can inspire action. In some smaller ways, or maybe bigger for some of you bold visionaries, we all can have a similar effect. Developing a story with facts and emotion can ignite us and others to make small Nudges that have a huge effect, but how do you build them?

How Do You Build Them?

When Christine and I first got involved with Story, our initial thoughts were something like, "What's the big deal? Isn't this easy to do? Haven't we been doing it a lot during our lifetimes?" Of course, the answer to those questions is a definite maybe! When we went to build our first few stories, we found out that to do it well, it took a little more effort than we thought.

I remember that one of the first stories I relayed to Christine was…pretty good? Christine is always positive, but I could see her facial expressions and may have even heard her thought bubble saying, "Okay, John, that was pretty interesting…. You certainly have some passion and energy, and I eventually got your point. But you seemed to ramble quite a bit, and it was very hard for me to follow the story. It worked, but I am a very patient listener and wonder how many other people will have the time and patience to get you?"

Since we deal with feedback together pretty well, I was able to tease these thoughts out of her and try to see her point of view. She told me I was not very crisp with some details, and I jumped from place to place in the story, which made it difficult to follow. Since I had not rehearsed my story, the "elephant" jumped in from time to time and made things worse. Even though the story made my point, I could do much better. Since I am curious and know about neuroplasticity, I started wondering, "What if it were crisper? What if a better story could make the point more effectively? Would more people be interested? What if I took several steps back and really began to work on this?"

So, Christine and I worked together on building our own Arsenal of Stories; we shared them with each other and customers, and then we evaluated and adapted them. It was fun, and we found that the more we did it, the better we became. We were turning our two-lane road into a superhighway. Developing stories became effortless over time, and we could even improvise them on the fly for the specific person and situation. It was a very rewarding experience.

Okay, so that was our experience with Story. Maybe you feel you are different and can already tell good stories and even ad lib one if you have to. You might be right, but that has not been our experience with our clients. Early on in our workshops, after the initial opening and discussion, we would have one of the company executives tell the Company Story. We do not want to criticize anyone and, truth be told, we admit this may not have been the best strategy. Letting an executive ad lib a story as a model for excellence was not our brightest idea, and quite honestly, was a bomb, which was our fault. So next, we decided to get a couple of the executives together before the workshop to rehearse the story. What we discovered was somewhat of the same thing. Yes, they could tell a decent story, but nothing compelling enough to move the other team members.

However, it was during one of these particular storytelling meetings that a tipping point occurred. We had seven senior execs in a very fast growing SaaS software company who were trying to use Story to accelerate their on-boarding process for new reps. Everyone in the room realized that his or her stories were not very good, but no one really wanted to voice that opinion. It got pretty uncomfortable in the room until one of the senior VPs just blurted out, "Hey, guys, let's just admit it. We are terrible at this."

We were ecstatic that a person with his accomplishments with six of his peers in the room could be so authentic and real. His story was probably the worst. However, his honesty led us to a real discussion about what it takes to build a great story and surfaced an even bigger concern. If they could not even do it—tell a compelling Company Story—how could they train and model it to new reps to help them be more effective, faster?

What would happen if they could build this story? Since Christine and I knew how to do this, we just suggested that we "slow down" a bit and build the story from the ground up, just like we would teach it in the workshop—a real case where "slowing down to speed up" would get them to the goal faster. So we stepped back and began building the story using our Story Building MAP™: Building Blocks with short phrases—both facts and emotions. The executives took turns telling it and got feedback each time to improve the story. It turned out to be both memorable and easy to tell. The story used the company's founder as the main character and really showed the vulnerabilities and struggles the company went through to become so successful.

The cool thing about that day was that everyone contributed, everyone left being able to tell the story, and everyone felt confident that this story would arm their people with a tool that would be a differentiating factor for customers—one much more effective than the hodge-podge of disjointed stories they had all started with. One of the great things about our customers is that they are smart and teach us things all the time, and we learned a valuable lesson that day. Now, we work with top executives before the workshop to help them through a similar process, ensuring that they will be able to tell a compelling story that their teams will want to adopt.

Christine facilitated the workshop at this company's sales kickoff with one of the executives telling this newly developed and rehearsed story. The new sales reps embraced it immediately, and then, another interesting thing happened. Debra, one of the senior salespeople, came up to Christine at the break and said, "That was one of the most valuable things I have ever gotten in my sales career at a kickoff meeting." Debra was excited that this leader could give her a valuable tool she could use the next day. After trying and mastering the use of story, Debra subsequently became a champion of using this skill to make stronger and more memorable points. This reaction cemented for us that if you want to make a big impact and cause Nudges and action, spend some time developing, revising, and rehearsing your stories.

But what is a good story?

What Makes an Inspiring Story?

In order to better understand this question, we had to take a step back and think about what makes up an inspiring story. Joseph Campbell gives a very detailed discussion of necessary story elements in his book, *The Hero's Journey*. During his life, he believed that the basics of story are similar, and that all great movies and books follow this path. As it turns out, he had a huge influence on the film industry. When do you listen fully and attentively, and when do you tune out because you have other things on your mind?

As you know, most inspiring stories have a strong character or "hero" with whom people can identify, and very early on you know what is going on, the Background/Beginning: Who is in the story and what is the current situation? If you, as the listener, can establish this information and feeling clearly, you start to identify with the hero and feel connected to what is coming.

Next, most good stories spend a bulk of the time on the Middle or Struggles. What is the struggle? Murder, divorce, love lost, children in trouble, the bad guys are coming, losing a key deal, a leadership problem trying to get people to change, etc. No matter what it is, it's the part where you start really getting sucked in or pushed out. Do you identify with the struggle? Is it believable? Of course, the interesting part is the impact on your new friend, the "hero." Will he get hurt? Will it ruin her life? Will it affect his children? Will she win something or lose something?

While listening attentively to the plot, you are trying to identify with the story and put yourself in the hero's shoes. Think about it. When you walk out of a movie or put down a book, it is most likely because you cannot relate to the hero or another main character. Therefore, you don't consider the struggle to be worthy of your attention. However, when it is worthy, you are captivated and can't pull yourself away. You feel like you are living the hero's journey. Again, this is the longest part of a good story, be it a fireside tale, a movie, a book, or a song. The teller weaves a mesmerizing tale of the struggles and how they affect the hero that leaves you sitting on the edge of your seat, saying, "Tell me more."

I remember the following scene from the movie *The Last of the Mohicans* like I just watched it yesterday.

The main characters are in a cave together. The snobby Englishman, Major Duncan Heyward, has been wounded. They are out of powder, and the only escape route from the enemy is to jump into a monster waterfall. Some jump and some stay. My elephant loves this scene and can recount it with a lot of facts and emotions. Of course, now we have reached the Tipping Point in the Story. This is the critical moment when the hero realizes he must do something different and make the decision to act that brings us to the Ending/New Beginning of the story.

In the movie, the good Indians jump over the waterfall and the bad Indians capture the girls. The fact that Hawkeye, the "hero," loves Cora, one of the captured girls, and wants to spend the rest of his life with her, has been building all during the movie. So naturally, Hawkeye tracks the bad Indians down and goes solo into their camp to make his argument against the villain, Magua, with the chief, for his newfound love, Cora.

The tipping point is usually shorter than the struggle, but it sets up the ending. It is this event—the bad guy has the girl—that makes the hero realize he will take action, leading to the new world order. The chief lets Magua have the other girl, burns the major, and lets Cora and Hawkeye walk into the sunset. If you saw the movie, you know there was a little battle in between where a few folks lost their lives, and that Hawkeye shoots the major from some ridiculous distance away, ergo Long Rifle, so he will not suffer in the fire. However, the bad guys capturing Cora, along with Hawkeye's speech to the chief, set it all up and lead to Hawkeye's idyllic life with Cora, and Chingachook becoming the "last of the Mohicans."

What if Hawkeye had not taken this risk? What if he had said, "Oh well, Magua has the love of my life and there's nothing I can do about it"? What if he didn't track down the camp and walk in solo, but headed back to civilization? I guess it might have had a different ending and James Fenimore Cooper would not have sold so many copies of his book. Luckily, Hawkeye took a different path of action.

The Ending, or New Beginning, was and is the shortest part of the story, and we remember it, too. In the movie, the good guys who are left are standing on a mountain overlooking the other mountain ranges. Hawkeye is hugging Cora and Chingachook is philosophical about being the "last of the Mohicans." It felt good after all the drama of the Beginning, Struggles, and Tipping Point. Sometimes the Ending can even become the beginning of the next story. Remember *Mad Men* Season 7? In the last episode of the season, Don Draper lets Peggy make the customer pitch by herself. She is fabulous and wins the account—solo for the first time—both a good ending and possibly a New Beginning for Season 8.

When Christine and I thought about great stories and what was happening within them, we realized that they were crisp. The content flowed seamlessly. There were good transitions. And we really identified with the hero and walked a mile in his or her shoes. We understood the struggle and the negative impact of staying there. The story was filled with both facts and emotions. Then, of course, the tipping point was simple and it ended. When we compared all that to my first attempt at story, we saw that the beginning was not quite as crisp. The hero was fuzzy, not clear. I really did not explain the struggle in a clear, concise manner that flowed. It was hard for someone else to understand the real impact on my hero, which begged the question, "Why does he even have to change?" The tipping point was okay, but I spent way too much time on the ending/new beginning.

Through our work, Christine and I have certainly learned from our own mistakes, but even more so, from our clients. We have noticed that it is difficult for our clients to describe the trajectory of a hero who pulls us in. This problem is especially true as it relates to customers developing their own stories of what they have gone through to get to where they are today. Christine reminds me that it is human nature to want to jump to the ending of the story, particularly when it is compelling, and forget or even deny the pain one went through to get there. It is human nature to want to project success, all we have accomplished, and all we are doing right, versus, where we have failed and gone wrong along the way. After all, being vulnerable—showing people our mistakes, warts, and flaws—is often perceived as the kiss of death in business, isn't it? Yet, just like a hero's journey, we don't relate to, or more importantly, don't *believe*, a Success Story, unless we understand the struggles one faced to create that success.

I remember this point being made very clearly one day when Christine called me to debrief after she finished conducting a Story Building session with a client, a renowned university and business school with which we work. When Christine called me, she sounded a little wound up; I could hear it in her voice. She started to tell me about how she was working with the heads of the undergrad and graduate school, the communications dean, the business development people, and some other key folks who had a tremendous amount of knowledge about the university's history and development. She said:

> John, you wouldn't have believed it…. I started
> by asking everyone in the room to take me back

to the beginning of the school's story and how it got its start. As they described their beginning, there was a clear hero and mission, and the university developed quickly into a local success. I said to them, "So tell me more," and they went on to say that the world of academics started to change and things got a little rough in the school's history. I said, "Well, that's really interesting; tell me more…," and then, John, I started to get frustrated because everyone kept brushing over the difficulties and jumping straight to the ending. They began touting what a great, successful, world-renowned school it is today that it is attracting talent from all around the globe. So then I said to them, "Hold on a second; let's go back to the struggle. Tell me more," and once again, there was some brief chatter, but they moved straight to the ending.

Honestly, John, it was as if they were running away from that period in their history. We went through this like four times. Well, then, you know me John, since they weren't getting me and how important it was to understand and share the difficulties they came from, I just looked at all of them and said very bluntly, "Look; here's the thing: nobody gives a crap about how great you are; they only care about what you went through to become great." Everyone just looked at me, dead silent, and I thought, *Did I overstep? Did I go too far?* However then, something shifted, and it was like magic. They really started digging in to what was going on during those difficult times and the frustrations the school experienced. So John, I think we got their story, warts and all.

Actually, telling all the great things that we have done to help our hero succeed is not all that interesting. In a good story, the listener identifies with the hero and asks, "What do I need to Nudge to make that happen?" It is natural that people start with the ending, or "new beginning," because that is the part that makes the most sense. However, the struggles in a story are the relatable content, the differentiator, and the credibility-builder, and our Story Building MAP™ (S.B.M.) helps develop them.

Our Story Building MAP™

We believe that the MAP we use to teach people effective Story Telling helps them over all of the natural hurdles. The MAP encompasses several building blocks: The Background/Beginning, The Middle/Struggles, The Tipping Point/Critical Event, and The Ending/New Beginning. (Please refer to page 138 for an illustration of our Story Building MAP™). We have already covered that the first step in TATN is knowing what you want and why, and if it is not yourself you are developing the story for, you must know whom you are trying to inspire toward action. What point are you trying to help your listeners see that they do not see now? Or how can they see and feel the impact of the changes in your hero and possibly identify with his or her actions to end the struggle? If your listeners can relate to the vulnerability and struggle, then they can more easily commit to their own Nudges.

Stories can make several points, such as: There's no place like home; evil witches don't win; and sometimes "All Powerful Leaders" are not exactly what they market themselves to be, in spite of the cool voice and curtain. It is okay to have a few reasons to tell a story or a few morals in a story. However, check yourself when you practice the story by asking the listeners to tell you what they thought the point was or is. If they do not get it, the point is not clear or you are telling the wrong story.

I recently told a story using a metaphor to Mitch, the CEO of a fast-growing software company, about leadership by saying, "You have hired six Doberman Pinschers, and now you have to take them for a walk." My intended point was that even though he had hired senior leaders and "A" players, Mitch still had to set the vision, get them working in a coordinated fashion, create synergy among their efforts, and sometimes break ties on resource allocations and conflicts. The point of my story seemed pretty clear to me, but Mitch objected vehemently by saying, "I do not want to take anybody for a walk. They should be running on their own." I was startled by his reaction, but I remained calm and said, "Tell me more."

After being curious and listening actively to what this story meant to him, I understood that the why was not clear, and he was still in the same place. I agreed with Mitch that these were "A" players and that they should be taking the vision and creating innovative operating plans. They did not need much coaching, and Mitch really wanted them to run to capture the market opportunity because time was their enemy. So when I told him to, "Take them for a walk," he freaked. His elephant told him a story that made him angry: "Have I hired the wrong people who need me to show them exactly what to do?" This certainly was not the reaction I was trying to get with my story.

However, because I now understood how his elephant interpreted my story, and the response it elicited, I was able to adjust with a different story. I knew Mitch had been a part of a championship hockey team, so I said, "This situation reminds me of the hockey team you captained in high school. You had some great 'A' players on that team who could really skate, pass, and shoot, and your coach was very active in organizing, developing plays, and working on team communication." Since Mitch had lived this story, and as a captain, worked very closely with his coach to make these things happen, my comment made a lot more sense to him. He totally got my point and realized that he now was the coach. Even though he had hired industry-leading players with great experience and track records, every management team needs good coordination and communication to create great results. Instantaneously, Mitch and I were more aligned. Now we could begin to have a discussion on actions he could take to Nudge the team.

I am sharing this instance with you because, even after using and practicing story for many years, Christine and I can still get it wrong sometimes, as I did. But we've learned to be flexible enough to adapt. The best story in the world is useless if you do not Nudge the person in the appropriate direction. Additionally, when you know more of the person's personal history, in this case, the fact that Mitch was the captain of his high school hockey team, it can help you develop a more relatable story to the situation and push the right buttons. This spark will then cause the listener to pivot and take different actions. So even if you are not perfect in Telling the Story the first time, shift to Gathering. Watch for reactions, remain curious, and listen so that you can adjust and unleash more potential. Tell me more.

The Background/Beginning

We start building a story at the beginning. Where does it start? Who are the characters? What are they doing? How are they feeling? This should not be a long, drawn-out history with every little detail, but rather provide listeners with enough information to gain understanding, interest, and have them step into our story. I am an avid reader, and I personally find some of James Michener's books hard to get through because he spends a lot of time on the background, and I get bored. So keep the beginning simple, choosing characters or a hero with whom the listener can identify.

Here are three examples of these famous story beginnings, including two we've already mentioned:

Any Given Sunday: Al Pacino as Tony D'Amato, a famous football coach with star players and on his last leg. Jamie Fox, "Steamin'" Willie Beamen, a smart upcoming quarterback making a difference, but on the coaches side or not? Cameron Diaz as Christina Pagniacci, a young female owner who is her own boss.

Braveheart: Mel Gibson as William Wallace, a young and worldly Scotsman returning to his clan. With the English firmly in control, Wallace falls in love with a beautiful, childhood sweetheart, Murron (Catherine

McCormack) who is killed by the English governor. Patrick McGoohan as King Edward I, the devious English king, is the enemy of Scotland's freedom.

When Harry Met Sally: Two college students, Billy Crystal as Harry Burns and Meg Ryan as Sally Albright, moving from Chicago to New York link up for a ride. They have interesting conversations about life and men and women. Deep down, they are attracted to each other. Their lives in New York continue to be intertwined with work, spouses, and events.

All of these famous beginnings left Christine and I wanting to learn more. (By the way, we did not forget about the really interesting dinner scene from *When Harry Met Sally* at Katz's Delicatessen in New York City. We have had a few meetings there ourselves just to get the real feel of that setting. The corned beef is awesome and you could try your hand at acting, if you are bold enough). Good beginnings pull us in, and get us interested. In the ones you love to watch and remember, the Background/ Beginning of the story keeps us patient enough to wait for the really good part, the Middle/Struggles.

The Middle/Struggles

Now, of course, the Middle/Struggles is the fun part to listen to that really draws us into the story, but it can be a challenging part on which to work when we attempt to build our stories. For some elephant reason, most of us want to breeze through this section, the Middle/Struggles. We do not want to develop it as clearly as we might, and a lot of time, we are very ineffective in helping the listener understand how the struggle affects the hero. Yet this is the most important part. Why is the struggle causing pain, stress, or anxiety? Is it because the water is rising in the stateroom?

This part of the Story Building MAP™ reminds Christine and me of a day we were using Story to facilitate deal analysis and deal strategy. We call this CCSA (Collaborative Customer Story Analysis.) Incorporating Story into reviewing deals is a really terrific way for teams to collaborate, learn, and share together. This process helps win deals, drive revenue, and accelerate team learning. During this particular session, we asked the sales team to describe the prospect's story based upon the meetings they had held to Gather it: Beginning, Struggles and impact on the people in the deal, and Tipping Point.

This client has a compliance solution for financial technology companies. The prospect the rep was developing the story about was a very large bank that had just been fined $12M for a trading violation. Wow, that will darn sure create some urgency to change. Get off this boat fast—it is going down. Well, the rep told the prospect's story pretty well, until he reported this part as the Tipping Point. The rep then proceeded to spend most of his time telling us why the company would win the deal and all of its great features. Apparently, the deal team thought this was big news and cause for early celebration.

Later in the facilitation, when people could challenge the rep's plan, one of the other senior guys said, "You are fooling yourselves. I read that article as well, and what that bank got fined for is a really big problem for it. It has nothing to do with what we do in compliance or our solution. This has a big impact on the people in your story, but it will not create a need for our system. As a matter of fact, if you bring up that event, they will think that either you do not understand the article or their business, or you are not the right people to help them. Additionally, this is a big risk to your project because they need to provide a solution for the problem that caused the fine in the first place. It may have higher executive sponsorship and a sense of urgency crowding out resources, budget, and priority from your project."

Talk about a bucket of cold water, but what terrific advice! I mean wouldn't you rather get that advice from a colleague in a safe environment where you can process it and adjust? Or would you rather just sail along, after spending a lot of time on the account, potentially looking dumb to the customer because you did not have a clear understanding of its business?

We have seen that reviewing deals with Story is really impactful. The real point Christine and I are making with this story is that the team did not fully understand the struggles or impacts on the key people. What was this $12 million fine for? How did it happen? Who would be affected? What negative thing would happen if it were not fixed? In our workshop for salespeople, we actually call this dilemma "Impatient Selling." People have a strong tendency to breeze through the Middle/Struggles and really not understand it with clear detail. We want to assume that we understand, our defense attorney comes out, and we launch into our solution: why we are great, and why we can solve the problem. Doing this too early can be very dangerous. Later, we will share more about the linkage of effective Gathering of the struggles with developing the full story.

When we tell a compelling story that really makes our point, we have developed the middle/struggles clearly and explicitly enough that the listener gets it and maybe even feels uncomfortable. If this turmoil can happen to Hawkeye, could it possibly happen, or is it happening right now, to me? We want our customers really to get into the story, and if we watch them curiously, we will see whether and when they light up. Can they feel the pain of the hero? Are they really identifying with the hero? How visceral and emotional is their reaction to the struggle?

Most of us can remember two sporting events that make this point: Joe Theismann, the Redskins quarterback breaking his leg against the New York Giants in RFK Stadium in 1985, and Louisville's Kevin Ware breaking his leg in an Elite Eight playoff game against Duke at Lucas Oil Stadium in Indianapolis in 2013. If you remember those events, you actually cringe when you read the words. If you did not see them, look for them on YouTube. The raw emotion sets our elephant on edge, and the realization of the potential impact gets our rider cringing about what life is going be like with this injury. Our neurons are wiring and firing, and most of us have relived these moments in the deep part of our submerged icebergs. When Ware's injury was replayed on the news, at first, only the reaction of his fellow players was shown. You could feel their raw emotions: shock, sadness, and dismay. Their faces and whole bodies told us more than any announcer's words could ever reveal. Then we watched the break. Those neurons burned that memory with indelible ink on a superhighway, and just the mention of it evokes those raw emotions again. Powerful stuff.

Now, what if you depicted the struggles in your story with such clarity and emotion that your listener could actually feel it? Would it be a good story? Would your listeners be sitting on the edge? Might they want to do something new to avoid that situation? Would you and your company be memorable? Tell me more.

The Tipping Point/Critical Event

If your listeners are with you at this point and all in, meaning they get both the facts and emotions of what is happening to the hero, and clearly understand why the hero needs to get out of this situation, then they are ready for the Tipping Point or Critical Event in the story. Although it may be a surprise to the listener how this occurs, it is no surprise that it is coming. We knew that Hawkeye would find Cora and get her back. However, we did not know that they might drown going over a waterfall or that the story Hawkeye told the chief would be so interesting and compelling. (Nice trick how Hawkeye got the English major to translate his speech into French for the chief.)

Thus, the tipping point may be a surprise on the specific details, but if you have a clear, concise story with a powerful and emotional struggle, everyone will know that some straw has to break the camel's back. If the tipping point is not obvious, you haven't been paying attention.

I'm sure the Egyptian President, Morsi, wished someone had been telling him the struggles of the Egyptian people before they mobilized thousands through social media, occupied Tahrir Square, and got him overthrown.

Now if your story has some major Disney potential, the Tipping Point may be inherently obvious and the listener expects it to come. Having said that, we still think this part needs to be explicit. In addition, this particular building block is often a great place to start when you are crafting your story. If you know your exact tipping point, it is sometimes easier to see what action you want to take, as well as how to backtrack to your Beginning and Struggles building blocks: What was going so wrong that you could not live with the status quo? Making the Tipping Point plainly clear is so important that we encourage our Tellers actually to say, "You know that Hawkeye cannot live with Magua taking the girl. He will have to get her back." Or in our CCSA Story: "The error rates for these compliance issues are just too high. This may result in a FINRA or SEC violation."

Making this part of the story apparent helps the listeners live out the danger and decide whether they want to avoid it or not. If the story is effective thus far, the listener will be engaged but may not connect with what specifically causes the Story Teller's hero to act. For example, the customer in the CCSA Story may say, "Hey, I get that Joe is concerned about FINRA and the SEC, but for us, it is all about growth." As rapidly as we are growing, and with the number of employees we have, we cannot continue to have this many insider trading errors." Tipping point, tipping point, tipping point. The rep can say, "So you are saying, that for your organization, if you continue to handle it the same way, you will not be able to grow as rapidly? Did I get you?"

When we are patient enough to develop the Struggles and impact on key people, telling the Tipping Point can be an influential force to Nudge people to action. We call this strategy "Patient Selling" because people love to buy into and decide to take their own actions, but they are not that keen to change when they perceive they are being told or pushed. This is why we developed The Art of the Nudge™ to be more like judo than karate. We want people to opt in because we understand them and they are inspired by our stories. It has been our experience that learning to be patient enough to develop the struggle fully, so the Tipping Point matters to the listener, is very effective. We want a Tipping Point strong enough to make them run to the lifeboats—a different action that will create a happy ending.

The Ending/New Beginning

The last building block of story development is the

Ending/New Beginning. When Christine and I started on our story journey with our "early adopter" customers, we thought this part was when we should tell them all about our features and benefits—beating our chests about how great we are. Well...not really. Although we must admit that touting features or benefits does make one feel good, it is not really as helpful or interesting. If we think about telling a story to cause people to take action and we want them to identify with the hero, what do they need to know about how that hero's story ends? You got it. They need to know that our hero changed course and took action that is making him or her more successful today.

The Ending/New Beginning has to put closure on the story and help our listener see that they too can be heroes. Do you think the Maine deserters were envisioning themselves fighting with Chamberlain and his 300 choice men? Did they feel needed by the colonel for a big battle where they could make a difference? Were some of them dreaming of being heroes? Well, the Battle of Gettysburg and the heroics that held Little Round Top definitely made all of them heroes, some of them even giving their lives. However, the point is that as the men lived vicariously through Chamberlain's story, they became something other than deserters. One hundred and fourteen out of one hundred and twenty people were inspired by Chamberlain's moving story to take a different action.

So, in our story endings, we have to talk about our hero, and how he or she will have a better life than in the background/beginning. If we have worked our magic up to this point in the story, it is the logical next step or Nudge for our listener to be thinking, "How do I do that? Can I get some of that?" or "How do I make that change? Where can I join up? Can you help me?" If we do this well, the Nudge is easy.

Vulnerability Is Key to Storytelling

Vulnerability is a key ingredient that leads to good storytelling, although it is a counterintuitive idea to most people because we are taught that being vulnerable shows weakness. However, struggles without real vulnerability are just not perceived as authentic, so they really do not hook the listener. We want to make sure we highlight vulnerability as it relates to the Struggles block of the stories you are telling about yourself or someone else. We want to belabor the point about struggle and the impact on people. We know how critical organizational and personal vulnerability is as we tell our stories.

The reason the struggle is so important is because it allows us to bring out vulnerabilities, which in turn, bring out humanness. This makes a limbic connection, elephant to elephant. When we want to relate to someone and gain his interest, it is much better if the person feels we are just like him, "warts" and all. There is a wonderful TED Talk by Dr. Brené Brown called "The Power of Vulnerability." As part of a ten-year research stint, Brown spent a lot of time diving into this very squishy topic. In her talk, she does a great job of explaining why we humans want to pretend that we are perfect. The crazy part of that pretension is that everyone else has his or her own warts, foibles, and imperfections too. Brown says, "We live in a vulnerable world," but we "numb vulnerability." She goes on to state that "we are the most in debt, obese, addicted, and medicated adult cohort in U.S. history" as we try to deal with our issues by attempting to escape from feeling or portraying vulnerability.

So "vulnerability" is something most of us want to stay far away from, but unfortunately, when we try to tell a story of perfection, what do you think neurons deep in the iceberg tell the elephant to do? Is it, "Hey, let's tell a story about all of our troubles and struggles and issues so people can really get into our personal space and understand how fragile we are right now and that we have just about had it"? Or do you think the elephant instead brings up to the surface the "I am perfect as well" story? I mean, those neurons are wiring and firing, and you can spin a wonderful story about how perfect you and your company are. So can I.

However, what happens if we show some vulnerability? What happens if we let our listener know we are human, too, and we make mistakes, too, but that it is okay because we catch them and adjust? Will the listeners be more empathetic? Will they think we are weaklings, or will they think we are real people who can be honest and straight with them?

I am reminded of one of our clients, who was slow to moving its software to a cloud offering. The company soon realized that being late in adapting to the cloud was ultimately hurting it and its customers. So the leaders began introducing a very thoughtful, innovative, and incremental way for their customers to get to the cloud with them.

As Christine and I spent time with this client, building its story, we got a lot of push back because the client did not want to divulge to its customers that it was late to the cloud. At one point, one of the client's marketing people even stated, "We were taught not to share our warts in front of customers." This was a very tense moment, and Christine could sense the conflict with the CEO and the team. Knowing how critical vulnerability is to an authentic story, Christine took the risk to say, "Well, you can choose not to tell them, but if they are as smart as you say they are, they probably already know that you are a little late since you are introducing this now and not four years ago." Pause, deep breath, ominous silence. Then, "By the way, your customers may be moving slower, too, because of all their infrastructure, and therefore, they can relate to your struggles of not being first to the market and appreciate your incremental approach." Do you think Christine was correct in helping this client see the power of being human in front of its customers? Well, the client did, and incorporated vulnerability into its story to make it compelling. We use vulnerability because it works.

On a more personal note, have you ever been out with friends and heard about perfect little Johnny—straight As, captain of the team, best looking in the school, most likely to succeed? After your elephant runs to the bathroom and throws up (unless, of course, you are a skillful rider), you come back and tell about perfect little Suzie. I don't know about you, but my wife and I have five wonderful children, and I can assure you, their growing up was not all peaches and cream. We had moving struggles, car accidents, drinking situations, and other stuff. However, I certainly would not want to tell any of that stuff after hearing about little Johnny. My story in response would have been about how amazing, great, cute, and perfect my children are.

How would you feel, and what story would or did you tell after you heard about Johnny? What happens when a salesperson or leader tells you how great he is? Do we really think that after hearing about how great we are, other people will want to tell you about the problems, issues, and vulnerabilities in their companies or their lives? We don't, but we also know that projecting perfectionism is what sales trainers and leaders have been taught.

Another story told to us by a workshop participant who used to work in a comic book store illustrates this point—that is, portraying perfection does not build connection—in an interesting way. It is a story about the American hero, Superman. When Superman was first introduced, the comic book was a bomb. However, the publishers thought they had created a story with a lot of potential, so they hired some behavioral marketers to conduct focus groups and find out what was wrong.

Well, it just so happened that no one could identify with Mr. Muscles and Perfection, who could fly and save the world. It was neat and all, but how could our elephant who knows all of our imperfections, identify with this perfect person? Neither you nor I could ever be like this hero, so who cares? Well, to solve this problem, one of the publisher's creative types came up with the archetype Clark Kent. He was awkward, geeky, and just human enough that we could get into the character. We could become Clark Kent and see ourselves transforming into this hero, Superman, who took action to save humanity.

This concept is monumentally important, and we want to be sure we are very clear here so you can feel the power of divulging vulnerability. We are not saying that competence (Superman) is not important to project. We are saying that if that is the only thing that others see and hear, with no vulnerability, no struggle, or no overcoming adversity, then they will not believe it or really identify with the hero in a visceral way. Remember, they not only want to know the good things you can do, but more importantly, the struggles and adversity you overcame to get there. If people feel you are more like them than Superman, warts and all, they can put themselves into your shoes and see themselves taking action to avoid that struggle.

It reminds Christine and me of a story about President Lincoln. Lincoln was pretty fed up with General McClellan because he and General Meade would not engage General Lee and end the darn war. Well, there was this general out in the West named Grant, who was winning some big battles. So Lincoln decided to make a change and put General Grant in charge. Partway through briefing his cabinet, someone cut him off by saying, "Sir, you cannot do that. General Grant has a terrible drinking problem." Lincoln paused and lowered his head, making the naysayer think he was reconsidering. Upon raising it, he smiled and said, "Great; find out what brand he drinks and give it to the rest of my generals who can't fight." Lincoln clearly knew that Grant had drinking problems. He also knew he was the best fighting general the Union had. Additionally, Grant was extremely popular with the common soldier and civilian, who knew he had some internal turmoil, too. So, warts and all, Lincoln promoted Grant, whose contributions helped re-unite the United States during the Civil War.

A famous saying by Winston Churchill makes this point about vulnerability: "There is no great man to his butler. And the joke is on the butler." Churchill's point is it is very easy to see people's weaknesses or vulnerabilities, and yes, we all have them. Great leaders and people developers recognize this point as well and hire/place people in positions to leverage their strengths. As Christine and I have seen time and time again, when you tell a story revealing some vulnerability and struggle that you have overcome, others identify with it more closely and believe more in your strengths and ability to help them. That vulnerability is key to storytelling works wonders because the elephant can identify at the subconscious, limbic level with our humanness, which can help someone believe what you believe.

However, what happens when we persist with our story of perfection? Your listeners will want to give you the same hogwash right back. They are on a beautiful boat with a fantastic stateroom. The TV and air conditioning are great, and they have just called out for a steak dinner. They will basically tell you, "No need for any of your stories about lifeboats and shipwrecks. No water has come into our stateroom yet. We are perfect and will just stay here, thank you."

Without vulnerability in our story, we will be ineffective, and perhaps worse, we could have saved people from a lot of pain and anguish. If they recognized the need to act earlier, would the struggle be harder or easier? Isn't that the whole point of a story? Getting people to feel the tipping point through someone else so they can take action earlier? Sometimes, or maybe most of the time, when we let a crisis develop until it is out of control, the consequences and negative implications are a lot worse. At least that is my and Christine's experience in our personal lives and with a lot of our customers. So we encourage the leaders we coach to get bad news early and try to shift things before it becomes a disaster. One of the best ways to do that is for leaders to reveal their vulnerability with a Lessons Learned Story, letting their teams know that no one is perfect.

However, if you do not share stories of your struggles and vulnerabilities with your leaders and teams, and instead, you act like Superman, how do you think people will want to portray themselves to you? Christine and I strongly encourage leaders who want to use The Art of the Nudge™ and Story effectively to let Clark Kent have an important part in their stories. Share your personal vulnerability or your company's. It will have a profound effect on the listeners, making them more open and likely both to believe you and to tell you their real stories when you ask for them.

When we develop a story well and give it powerfully, "It just works," so repeat it often.

Give It Early and Often

After we develop our story, we have to give it in many forms, often, and with conviction. By repeating our story to ourselves and others with emotion, it will start to re-groove the dirt road and quickly turn it into a superhighway. A compelling story affects the limbic brain and how we feel, and that will lead to action. We have to be prepared to tell the story in many ways because as the amount of time we have and our audiences will differ. We do know that for most humans, the normal attention span is three to five minutes, so longer stories will have to become dialogues. Yet, through repetition, practice, and emotion, the compelling stories we tell have the power to make a difference, and they will.

This is another point where understanding our core personality and the personality of the person we are giving the story to can really be helpful. If we are fast-paced and outspoken, while our listener is detailed and reflective, we might want to slow down our usual pace and highlight specific facts. (Remember the "John and Jess Story.") However, if our listener is fast-paced and outspoken, we may want to tell a shorter, more pointed story, or an anecdote or metaphor. Christine and I have seen how just being cognizant of the different personality types and how each likes to process information allows us to make a slight adjustment in how we give the story, which, in turn, has a monumental effect on how the person receives it. The more important the interaction, the more important it is to take the time to prepare. Develop your story fully (Story Building Blocks), understand the person to whom you are telling it (personality profile), and rehearse it before going on stage.

Giving the story effectively plants seeds that take time to sprout. People need time and space for the elephant and rider to internalize the new vision and take action. Remember, change is hard, so it will be easiest to take the next logical step for them. What is that step? How do we nudge them toward it? And how do we help them nudge themselves?

An Army study was done after the Vietnam War on leg amputees, showing that it takes twenty-one days of repetition to begin laying the pavement on a dirt road. Your elephant has to internalize that we are not going down the old superhighway anymore, but venturing onto a brave new dirt road. Scientists know this because most of us get up during the night for needed bodily functions. For the first twenty-one days, an amputee will swing out of bed and fall flat on the floor. How could he not know remember that he is missing a limb? The rider gets it, but that darn elephant is following the old superhighway.

The researchers in this study and others observed that after twenty-one days, both the conscious and subconscious brain had internalized the new reality and pivoted. In this case, the amputees automatically reached for their crutches before getting out of bed. The point is that we have to be prepared to reinforce our story strongly for twenty-one days. As the rider gently and emotionally nudges the elephant, it will start to realize where we want to go and start its own nudges. If you want to succeed, give it a lot of nudges, in many ways, and daily for the first twenty-one days.

Once we have decided what we want and why (TATN Step 1), understood the stories being told (Step 2), and developed and told effective and inspiring stories multiple times and in multiple versions (Steps 3 & 4), what now? We'll show you in the next chapter.

Chapter Reflections

1. Developing a good story can have a huge effect upon inspiring us and others to action. *Colonel Joshua Chamberlain Story.*

2. Every good story has a natural progression that can be learned by following our Story Building MAP™ (S.B.M.) to increase effectiveness. It has a beginning, middle, and end.

3. Starting with the Beginning helps the story unfold naturally through the Middle/Struggles, Tipping Point/Critical Event, and Ending/New Beginning. It will be coherent and easy to follow.

4. A good story has a balance of both facts and emotions. The facts will engage the rider (the neocortex), and the emotions and the drama will engage the elephant (the limbic brain), making the story memorable. Telling a story with emphasis on the struggles will capture the imagination of the listener.

5. Vulnerability is a critical ingredient in any story, as it makes the hero both human and relatable. When a listener relates to the story, he steps into the story being told or is reminded of his own similar story. Either way, the listener is inclined to open up and share his story, creating a real dialogue. *Clark Kent versus Superman.*

6. One story doesn't fit every situation. Having multiple versions of your stories will allow you to adjust according to the listener, the time, and the situation. Good stories are repeated often to continue to inspire yourself and others.

Nudges

1. Think of a story you told effectively and put it in our Story Building MAP™ with facts and emotions.

2. Think of a leadership situation you are currently facing where you need to Nudge. Build a story for those listeners that will have them thinking in a new way.

3. Go tell that story to several people and get feedback.

TATN Step 5: Evaluate, Celebrate, and Adapt; Continue the Journey

Christine and I have talked a lot about the story of our Tipping Point. It led us to move full steam ahead, working together with our current clients with the active goal of helping more clients jointly and quickly. One of the Nudges we knew we would have to take was to clarify our website and become more prominent with our marketing activities. This step seemed pretty clear and like an easy one to take, so we marched ahead boldly with a new website design and marketing company. After the first few meetings, the completion of much of their work, and what we hoped was progress, we began to experience struggles. I felt things were taking too long and we were spending too much time on getting our content perfect. Christine was frustrated with the pace as well, but more willing to give it time to "work itself out."

As cash dripped out the door, feeding this Nudge with very little result, the tension between us began to rise, consuming a lot more of our time and conversation. It was frustrating and maddening to both of us, and soon it reached a boiling point. I brought it up in a very negative way, blaming us, our vendor, and the lack of progress. All true. Christine was calm enough to say, "Why don't we slow down a bit?" We then asked, "What would we recommend one of our clients to do at this point in a Nudge?"

This great question caused us to shift, realizing, "We are where we are." Complaining about what has not been done will not help. What we really needed to do was sit down and try to evaluate this Nudge—what was really going on, and how we need to adjust and adapt. Duh. We are somewhat embarrassed to admit that we made this mistake by rushing to an answer that we did not yet have. However, we also are faced with the realities of our fast-paced world. We try to accomplish too many things, too fast. We are bombarded by shifting priorities and social media, and sometimes, we just don't have the time to stay on top of things.

Our candid evaluation of our progress was rather startling. Although we had set some outcome measurements, we had not really discussed interim indicators or milestones. We really had no guideposts for us to discuss this Nudge in a factual, collaborative manner. This resulted in our elephant's feelings and emotions surfacing, without a skilled rider to steer. We also realized that as time progressed, our *what* and *why* had shifted as well. We were really expecting different outcomes in different timeframes than we relayed to our website company. So we went back to Step 1 of TATN, redefining our what and why and realigning our story and actions from there. It took a little more time, but for us, this evaluation process helped get us back on track, possibly averting an even bigger disappointment.

With that in mind, our last step in the process is to be constantly evaluating actions, interim milestones, and results. We need to adopt a learning culture and attitude. Celebrating small successes will build upon itself, motivate continued performance of those actions, and encourage others to try the same. For some reason, success is contagious—if it is real success. Just giving ourselves trophies for showing up might not lead to achieving our what and why. However, if we have some indicators of success and do them well, we should celebrate. If it is a milestone or result that everyone can see, we should really celebrate and share it, encouraging more of this behavior and action. In order to celebrate effectively, though, we have to spend some time clearly understanding what the outcome measurement of this Nudge is, and what interim indicators would indicate we are making progress.

Christine and I have worked in many different organizations over the years, and it is our common experience that most executives and leaders intellectually understand that evaluating progress and celebrating success is an important, even necessary, task. It is also our experience that celebrating success is one of those things that hard, charging, goal-oriented people/executives struggle to implement, probably because they do not take the time to celebrate their own interim successes along the way.

Christine relayed a story to me once of when she was working with Tony, the CEO of a biologics company. Tony was thirty-six when he was handed the keys to the company from the previous CEO and told, "We are just about out of cash; the company is yours if you want to try to revive it." Six years later, Tony had raised venture capital, built the company to 100 million, and taken the company public. At this point, Tony and his team, with much anticipation from the medical and investor community, were in the process of getting ready to launch their "hallmark" product that they had developed, manufactured, and just received FDA clearance for. They had worked tirelessly on planning the annual sales meeting to launch the product effectively to their national sales team.

Christine had been coaching Tony and some of his team, so she attended the sales kickoff meeting. She described the sales team as exhilarated. Tony and his VP of Commercial Operations had both given inspiring speeches during the dinner that were incredibly well-received, and the product meetings were a huge hit. The team was ready and excited to hit-the-ground-running in a couple of months, as planned. The meeting ended on Sunday morning, and Christine, Tony, and other members of the organization flew home together Sunday afternoon, feeling great and on a bit of a high.

The next day, Monday afternoon, Christine was meeting with Tony and started by saying, "Congratulations." Tony responded, "For what?" And Christine said, "Well, that was an incredible meeting." Tony replied, "What meeting?" Christine: "The National Sales meeting." Tony: "Oh yeah, that, well that was yesterday. I have already moved onto the next goal." Maybe this wasn't achieving an outcome measurement, but it was an interim success that could have been celebrated.

We often use the analogy of golf to explain the importance of interim measurements. The outcome measurement of golf is your score—total shots per round, measured per hole with pars, birdies, eagles, bogey, and double bogeys—to beat your opponent or handicap. However, anyone who has played or watched golf knows that thinking about the score when you are executing pulls you away from the flow. Instead, golf pros try to execute subconsciously. They try to visualize the shot and just let their muscle memory take over. How do they know whether they are on the right track? Certainly, they can see where the ball goes and what kind of shot they hit, but how can they know whether this will lead to victory? You got it, interim measurements. For golf, those measurements are number of fairways hit, number of times on the green in regulation, and number of putts. By counting these interim results, golfers will know whether they are having a good or bad day. They will try to adjust what they can. And they will celebrate both interim successes, which should happen more often, and the ultimate victory, if achieved.

When coaching sales managers to higher performance, we help them chart their Buyer's Process MAP, identifying the critical steps in the process where they really help the customer better than their competitors do. We encourage them to evaluate the times when they execute those milestones because we know that doing enough of these critical activities will lead to more wins. Additionally, we, of course, want them to celebrate in some meaningful way when they win deals—both the win and the key actions taken. Not only will other reps get excited about these wins, but they will start to believe they can win, too, and take their own Nudge to model these behaviors and outcomes.

Christine and I believe very strongly in measurements: both outcome and interim, driven by required activities. It is our experience in the training industry that too many training initiatives are launched without any clear linkage to business outcomes, and certainly, no clear plan to track and measure the impact on the business. We believe that most training projects should be a tool to accelerate a specific business initiative, which has clear business outcomes: increasing revenue, increasing profit or cash flow, enhancing customer satisfaction for referrals and increased revenue, increasing employee engagement to increase productivity, all leading to increased shareholder value. Process and functional improvements are necessary to do this as well as the work activities related to them.

Since it is a pet peeve of ours, and we know our clients will get more value and good feedback if they do this, we encourage all teams making continuous improvements or innovations to establish both outcome measurements and interim measurements or milestones. Develop them in a collaborative environment with input and agreement and then track and report on them regularly. This way, everyone on the team can engage in dialogue about what is shifting and discuss the cause and effect. We should be celebrating successes that lead us and others to continue to do more of the same. If we are not hitting the interim milestones, we should rethink our actions and adapt them so we can hit the milestones, leading to the final outcome.

Without thinking of and executing this step with some rigor, we truly will not know whether we are doing the right things or...just doing things. It may take a little time by slowing down, but we know that it will serve us all better in the end as we go on our journey to pave a dirt road, ultimately getting there faster. Christine and I realize that this can be daunting, so we have developed a way to help customers think through this to make it both specific and simple. Hitting milestones and celebrating successes become powerful stories with heroes that others in your organization will want to emulate.

We love the story of Roger Bannister (adapted from his autobiography, *Twin Tracks*), the first four-minute miler, for two reasons. The first one is that many runners, including Glenn Cunningham, had been trying for decades to break the four-minute mile barrier. For some reason, Roger believed he would be the man to accomplish this goal, and he developed a powerful and emotional story to motivate himself. He saw himself breaking this record, and he envisioned the cheering crowds. He let himself feel the emotions of elation, pride, satisfaction, and the humility of accomplishing this goal. He then repeated the story relentlessly as he trained, overcoming all the obstacles in his mind of why he or any human could not achieve this goal. His strong why and story fueled his tenacity and courage to persist in the face of many races where he did not break the record. He kept adapting his techniques and improving his training, until finally, on May 6, 1954, he smashed this barrier.

The second reason we love this story is that we believe it substantially impacted other runners. In the weeks following this historical event, it was reported in newspapers worldwide for everyone to see, hear, and marvel about. Most read it and thought, "I could never do that." However, some brave souls' elephants and riders came up with a different belief and question: "Why not me?" And yes, two months later, another pair of milers accomplished this same goal, as would many more in the ensuing years. Do you think they were inspired by Roger? Was it a "Nudge" in the running world that caused other runners to see that if Roger, their hero could do it, maybe they could as well? Did they lay awake at night dreaming of that race, seeing the faces of the crowds, and feeling the same feelings of elation and pride?

We definitely think so, and like you, we have seen many

similar examples in our personal and professional lives—examples where some improvement or break-through occurred, was celebrated, and affected the be-liefs of others who, subsequently, achieved the same breakthrough. This situation leads us to believe that, of-ten in our lives, it is good to be a follower and to copy or model the person, process, or company that is already achieving what you wish to achieve. What story can you build that has you both emulating someone initially and then surpassing him? Of course, it is easier to emulate than to innovate, but we also know that our powerful brains can overcome many situations and challenges. Many times, innovation is the Mother of Necessity. If we are evaluating our measurements and not achieving, we have untapped ability to innovate; we can invent the tools, processes, or actions that will get us to a New Be-ginning. Innovation is the gift of mankind, and every one of us has an infinite power to do it if we want to and will put ourselves in the struggle.

As we embark on a Nudge, be it personal or organiza-tional, we need to keep evaluating and celebrating both interim and outcome measurements. Evaluation will provide a guidepost to understanding constantly where we are, what more we have to do, and how to adapt the Nudges to overcome the potholes and persist long enough to get us to the end goal—the *what* that answers the *why*. Through this constant learning and reinforcement, we make big changes happen with small steps and incremental progress. THE ART OF THE NUDGE.

Understanding Practical Uses of TATN

Christine and I began this journey by first using these tools ourselves. We used them both personally to take action, and as consultants in working with our clients for greater business success. It struck us that most of what we do as leaders is influence new actions, and in order to do that, we have to gain alignment from our teams so they can buy in and take cascading actions to make things happen. We think the true test of leadership is to look around you. If other followers are going on your journey with you, then you are a leader. We also believe that effective leaders are constantly looking for new and better ways to increase their own and their business's performance, new products, new ways of distribution, new ways to innovate processes, and new ways to lead people.

In *The Work of Leaders* by Wiley Publishing, Vision, Alignment, and Execution, or VAE is discussed (Straw, et al.). VAE is the work leaders must do to make improvements for increased performance; that work includes: creating an inspiring vision that people want to be a part of, gaining alignment on this vision so people will want to take action, and putting execution plans in place to make these dreams become reality. We believe in this view of leadership and know that individually and organizationally, it is hard to pave over the old superhighways and create new ones out of dirt roads.

We have struggled ourselves with taking new action and leading initiatives. And we have seen leaders at all levels get stuck on one or multiple parts of this work. We believed that The Art of the Nudge™ Communication Framework and the complementary tools discussed in this book—Personality Profiles, Story, and Nudges—might help leaders on this journey. So we then began introducing them to our clients. We did so, initially, to discover what they really wanted and why. Then, to help them craft Nudges, both personal and organizational, to help them pivot and take different actions. This process was done in workshops to immerse and socialize numbers of other team members who could co-learn and collaborate to make those Nudges, as well as one-on-one, dependent upon the phase and situation.

We were getting a lot of good feedback from our customers such as, "Your workshop was impactful, helping us Nudge our culture and getting leaders to buy in to and begin executing change"(Sue, CEO); "Our sales teams loved building and telling customer stories, and it has already helped us win several deals"

(Jeff, VP of Sales); "I personally consulted with Christine on how to build my strategy story to deliver to our analyst community about the company's direction. It was crisp, clear, and very effective, and we saw both an increase in coverage of our firm and a slight bump in stock price" (Pete, CEO Public Software Company); "I was amazed at how differently my colleagues have been interacting with me now. I have slowed down my pace when needed; I am applying Gathering skills first, and then telling compelling stories to get them to see and buy into a new way" (Laura, VP Marketing, SaaS Software Company). We also were getting very high reviews on the workshops themselves and how engaged and inspired the participants were.

With all of this positive feedback, you can imagine our surprise when at the end of several workshops we would get the question, "We get that these are useful planning and communication tools to create action, but when exactly do we use them?" At first, we were taken aback by this question because the answer is "Most of the time." We also thought we had given enough clear examples in our workshops that the answer should be apparent. But because we use our own process, we know that when we hear something startling, it is time to slow down and become the curious detective, not the objection-handling defense attorney. One of the simplest and most effective questions in these situations is, "What do you mean? Tell me more." Pause, take a deep breath, relax, and move to Gathering skills. Try really to understand their struggle and blockages. What is keeping our new heroes from going forth and slaying dragons with these new tools?

Our clients are smart, so we really listened and processed the feedback. We realized it may not be intuitively obvious to everyone reading this book or taking our workshop about how and when to use these tools. It would be like knowing how to play the piano but not recognizing when a piano was around, or when it might be appropriate to play; maybe the piano skills did not help you that much.

So we took a step back and tried to clarify. These are planning and communication tools to help us take sustained, decisive action for new achievements. They will help us define the Nudges/actions and create the buy-in or alignment to veer down a new dirt road. As leaders, we need tools for Vision, Alignment, and Execution, and they need to work together to create outcomes. So, in a simplistic manner, The Art of the Nudge™ (TATN) is a strategic communication framework to help us think, plan, and take action. Once we know what we want to do and why, we can use the Story Engine, Personality Profiles, and Nudges to ensure we are successful. If it is a personal Nudge, we really have to spend time Gathering our own story. What is the story we are telling ourselves that drives the feelings leading us to act this way? Once we know that story, we can craft another one that is inspiring and compelling to take us on a new dirt road. If we are Nudging another person, we must at least Gather his or her story. If we are Nudging a large group or organization, it becomes multi-faceted. We must Tell and Gather upfront so we know enough about people's impediments, blockages, and the superhighways they are traveling in order to craft a new story that will inspire them to come with us, take a risk, change their current thinking, and take action. As always, we need a feedback loop or process for hearing reactions so we can gauge the success of the actions our story is eliciting, then learn and adapt.

If you are planning to make shifts or pivot as a leader, we recommend that you use the TATN Framework and take the time to go back to the Beginning. Many of us in this fast-paced digital society will ask, "Why slow down? We have already built an Arsenal of Stories. Can't we just tell our stories and move quickly?" Yes, it definitely is how we are conditioned, but do we have the time to slow down just a little and make sure we get it right to help us speed up? It happened to Christine and me in the marketing story we related earlier, and remember the "Walking the Dobermans" story? What if I, John, had slowed down just a bit to gauge whether that was the right story? What if I had come up with the "Hockey Team Story" earlier? Would it have hit the mark better and removed the need to take two steps back? We think it is prudent advice for you and us to start with NUDGE: 1. Knowing what we want and WHY, and, 2. Understanding the current story or stories being told.

We have all heard stories of leaders who started new initiatives and failed. Most of the time, they decided quickly, without really knowing what they wanted and why or understanding the current stories being told in that situation. Without this key planning data, they marched off courageously anyway, trying to change something they either weren't committed to or they really did not understand. And by not "slowing down" a little and doing some strategy or planning, it turned out that they were either not persistent enough to re-pave the new dirt road and/or close off the old super-highway, or they just plain underestimated how much cement, macadam, and gravel it would really take.

The tools we have outlined in this book can help create new momentum and guide action to achieve the potential of your people and organization. So we thought some specific customer examples might also help answer the question of when to use them. Hopefully, as we describe these real-world situations, you will relate and begin to think of your own opportunities and struggles, and where/how to apply TATN to help you.

Nudge Type 1: Using Story to launch a new product to drive revenue growth

The simplest example we have is of a client, Kate, who was the head of training for a successful high-growth digital media company with multiple product lines. Kate was an early adopter and understood how story could be a powerful tool to help her company launch a new product at a kickoff meeting to start the year. A lot of hope and excitement existed for this product to be embraced by the sales team and then adopted by current customers to drive add-on revenue and hit growth targets. The struggle was that the senior team could not agree on the correct positioning and exactly how to discuss it with their sales force.

Kate invited us to partner with her and spend time with the senior team. Naturally, we told our story and gathered the team's story. We really wanted to understand the implication of this product being successful or not, and we wanted to know what the senior team was debating with its current plans. After a lot of Gathering, it became evident that the positioning was not clear or agreed upon. We believed that building a Company/New Product Introduction Story would be useful, and if we could jointly build a story that was both emotional and factual, it would be a great tool to roll out to the sales force.

Although skeptical, the senior management team members spent the time understanding the power and mechanics of story and working through the iterative story-building process. Yes, they struggled with vulnerability, but ultimately, they built a really good and human story about their company and new offering. With Kate leading the charge to ensure the vision and message was clear, Christine conducted a workshop to launch this new story with the overall concept of Gathering. The interim measurement we agreed upon was: Could the sales team accurately Gather and reflect its customer's story with emphasis on the Struggles and Tipping Point, both individually and organizationally? The key activities were for each rep to be able to give the new product story to open up his or her customer and then Gather that customer's story. The outcomes, which are still being measured, are an increased, qualified pipeline, leading to more won deals and an increase in new product revenue.

Nudge Type 2: Augmenting a sales methodology to continue fast revenue growth

Another client we've helped is SCRA (South Carolina

Research Authority), a $300 million applied research and development company that commercializes technology in complex partnerships. A new dynamic CEO, Bill, was brought in seven years ago to inject new leadership practices and create leverage with the great foundation that the founders had built. Since the company's solutions were extremely complex and often sold to the government, it needed very experienced, smart, and technical people who did not see themselves as salespeople. One of the things Bill did was train all of the company's people on selling—both Strategy and Execution. Over the years, it helped and was implemented fairly well, but more recently, it seemed to be languishing. SCRA engaged us initially to see whether we could help it introduce a new methodology.

After some long Gathering sessions, we heard the company leaders really say that what they wanted was to continue using their R.A.D.A.R. sales methodology from The Complex Sale, but to turbocharge it.[2] One of the most

---

2 If you are leading sales and already use a sales methodology, you may be wondering what our view is on this and how we fit in. We believe that TATN is critical to execution, and it can be layered on top to accelerate specific business outcomes. The tools of both Story and Personality Profiles can augment the effectiveness of your existing methodology, especially as you roll out significant new initiatives. We have already augmented the following sales methodologies: Sandler, Challenger, Solution Selling, R.A.D.A.R., and Power Base, among others—both tactical and strategic selling methodologies. Story Gathering skills help sales teams gather customer insights and collaborate more effectively. We are not a replacement system or in conflict with these sales methodologies, but we will, in effect, turbocharge their usage.

effective things they believed the sales managers did was deal reviews, and they also believed they had many, many customer stories in the company's institutional memory that were not being leveraged. Based upon what we Gathered, we recommended that they energize their current system with story skills. We conducted workshops to help them learn how to Gather and catalog powerful Customer Stories that could be shared effectively across regions, deals, and industries. We showed them how to integrate Telling the prospect's story into their deal reviews, called CCSA. The sales leaders were relieved that we helped them realize they did not need to rip and replace their existing sales methodology, but could instead turbocharge and leverage the investments they had made with R.A.D.A.R. over the last six years. They also found that layering story skills into their current sales system removed the stigma of selling by allowing them both to feel and act in a consistent and authentic manner, in line with their belief in customer service. This technical sales team was happy and energized with this supplemental approach. Bill stated that this injection was a strong factor in recording another record year with the largest backlog of revenue in the company's history.

Nudge Type 3: Enhancing leadership effectiveness by Nudging the culture

We were also enlisted to help a large non-profit organization that raises monies and awareness for blood cancers, with the ultimate goal of finding bone marrow matches for people that suffer from these cancers. Chris, the CEO, was incredibly passionate about the company's mission and purpose, but he was feeling stuck and uncertain of what to do. The company's growth had become stagnant, and the current company culture had a lot of toxicity, largely due to a former management team member.

Chris was introduced to us through one of Christine's trusted advisors and former colleagues. During their initial discussion, Chris described that there was misalignment between Chris, his leadership team, and the employees. People were unhappy, not selling effectively, and clearly not motivated. Chris believed that if he just trained his managers on basic management blocking and tackling, they would be able to root out non-performers. He asked Christine whether we could train his leaders on tactical/basic management strategies (i.e., teach them how to handle difficult employees and manage out those who were not performing).

Christine asked Chris whether he could take a moment to slow down, go back, and share the three most important things he was hoping to accomplish with this training. Chris responded with: "First, I want all the leaders and employees to share my passion and belief in this company and what we are doing; second, I want to collaborate with my leaders to define a culture and work from the ground up to re-build the culture together; and third, I need to grow this business through better sales and messaging." As Chris listened to himself clearly defining the outcomes of what he wanted, he realized the training he had envisioned was not going to achieve these objectives. As Christine and I discussed and brainstormed how we could help him, we rolled out a tailored leadership workshop to help his team members understand both their company and their personal *whys*. The goal was to help them define a more appropriate culture to keep the company growing.

One of the potholes along this new journey was that Chris, who happens to be German, was viewed by his team members as "emotionally removed," and they were a little fearful of him. However, after Chris told his personal story of "Why I Do What I Do," his team learned of all the hardships and sacrifices Chris had made to follow his passion. They were inspired by his strong belief in helping others through business. Because Chris shared some very vulnerable parts of himself throughout his story, each leader did the same. This sharing resulted in a much stronger bonding and aligning, leading them to work on building their Company Story, including the cultural attributes they wanted to create. This experience turned out to be a catalytic event for Chris and his team, and today, they are committed to cascading this culture in order to help them drive growth and, ultimately, help the cancer patients they serve.

Nudge Type 4: Using Story Gathering for constructive conflict resolution, disagreeing agreeably, and better collaboration

One of the companies mentioned in this book that we work closely with, Tozour Energy Systems, has a tremendous commitment to leadership development. It takes a lot of actions to ensure that leaders at all levels, as well as individual contributors, have a focus on growth both for their current roles and future roles/career development within the company. The President, Kevin, and the Executive VP, Frank, commit dollars every year to individual and team coaching to help people learn "how" to work more effectively together while doing their work at hand. They utilize personality profiles to understand themselves, their teammates, and their customers, and they have engrained the use of this tool in their company culture. They have committed to training their sales and customer service teams, as well as leadership at all levels, on our Story Gathering.

After one of the workshops, Christine was working personally with Frank and one of his managers, Marcy, on her professional development, with the ultimate goal of having her become the successor in a critical leadership role. Christine described that the feedback discussion was going very well. Marcy was open to hearing Frank as he provided her with both positive and critical feedback in a very direct, but caring manner. However, Christine noticed that the pace and tone of the meeting changed dramatically when, at one point, Frank gave feedback that "hit quite a nerve." Marcy's body language, tone of voice, and pace of speaking all ramped up very quickly as she became defensive. In that moment, Marcy exhibited the "dominance factor" that had been clearly reflected in her personality profile. She became argumentative with Frank, saying, "I just don't agree with you Frank; that's not true!" Christine could see the exchange unfolding like a pre-written play. As soon as Marcy challenged Frank, he in turn matched her body language, tone of voice, and pace of speaking, challenging right back with, "Marcy, it is true; you just don't see it."

The formerly collaborative and positive dialogue quickly turned into a two people talking at each other and arguing. Christine let this go on for a few moments and then intervened by saying, "I need you both to stop for a minute and think about what we practiced in the workshop about Gathering the story and seeking to understand first. Marcy, do you even know why Frank thinks this about you?" Marcy responded, "No," and then smiled. Christine continued: "Now, instead of disagreeing with Frank's feedback, please use the 6 Gathering Questions™ to find out his story and his why and then reflect what you heard and ask whether you understand him."

Marcy started by asking Frank to take her back to the beginning, which Frank did. She then responded with "Tell me more," "Hmm," and so on. After she got Frank's entire story, she reflected it back to him, and said, "Do I get you?" Frank, with relief said, "Yes, you do," and went on to say, "You know, Marcy, the reason I want you to be aware of this area of development is because we are very much alike. We know this from our personality profiles, and I have made this same mistake too many times in my career. I want to spare you stepping on the same landmines as I have."

This conversation was a real breakthrough in their relationship. We know it may have taken a little more time to slow down and get there, but Christine has subsequently observed that this one small use of Gathering, which helped to de-escalate, foster insight, and create mutual respect, has improved their relationship and Marcy's performance. Frank and Marcy continue to utilize and practice this Gathering approach when they are discussing issues between them. This approach to dialogue has ultimately cascaded to their direct reports, avoiding some unnecessary friction and loss of productivity.

Many organizations feel that conflict resolution is a "squishy" subject that does not have a huge impact. Peg Neuhauser, in her book *Tribal Warfare in Organizations,* does a great job of outlining how to quantify the effect of this issue in companies. She relates that managers spend anywhere from 25-60 percent of their time resolving conflicts among and between "tribes." This issue crowds out time they could be spending on improvements to increase revenue, reduce cost, or improve customer satisfaction. If a company had 100 managers making $80,000 per year and we used a conservative estimate of 25 percent of their time, the total cost to the company would be $2,000,000 annually (3-4).

What executive or leader would like to have this time better deployed to create value? Furthermore, what if even more time than this was spent by mid-level managers and high level executives? Thinking of conflict resolution in this business outcome way puts a much different light on the subject than, "Oh well, that is just Richard and Bill. They don't get along," and it might be something to consider for your organization.

We find that managing conflict is one of the toughest situations for leaders in their interactions with subordinates, peers, and their managers. A Gallup research poll shows that conflict is abundant in our world and that the most effective leaders have skills to resolve conflict collaboratively. That said, it is not easy, but if you only use our Gathering tool for this situation, we can promise that you will be more effective, less stressed, and a lot more successful.

So we have just told you four stories of practical applications to using TATN. What we think is consistent about these stories is that they are real-life examples of using one or all of our tools as a catalyst for improvement or innovation. These stories are just a few ways our clients have used Nudges, and we are sure you will think of many, many more, but how do you practice and reinforce?

Continuing the Journey: 7 Steps to Reinforce

We think that by now all of you are clear that we travel our superhighways easily and dirt roads not so well, and if we want to build a new skill or use a new tool (taking the dirt road), then we have to put enough effort into the change to make it stick.

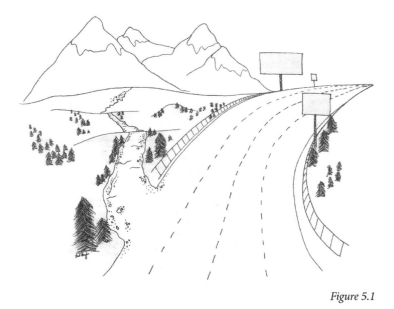

Figure 5.1

We think it is easier to do this for yourself and with teams using Nudge—the next logical step on the journey. Throughout our work, we have discovered seven recommendations for things you can do to help you along this journey:

1. Team with a partner to start and continue practicing TATN.

2. Identify your top three Nudges and both Gather your current story and develop an inspiring one that moves you to action.

3. Use our Story Gathering and Story Building

MAPS for focused practice.

4. Practice three times daily for the first twenty-one days (i.e., run through TATN for something you are planning, tell a Company or Customer Story and gauge the reaction; or Gather a prospect's story and reflect it back to see whether you "got them."), starting to pave a new Dirt Road.

5. Practice two times daily for the following thirty days (filling in potholes), so the macadam is laid.

6. Practice once a day for thirty days (you should be well on your way to a superhighway).

7. Congratulate yourself on achieving milestones, celebrate success, and repeat these steps.

With intentional practice of this system and these skills, your dirt road will become a superhighway. Your rider will have been nudging the elephant to take this road. And now that it is paved, the elephant will travel down the superhighway on its own, "in the flow." Your rider will only have to hold the reins lightly because the rider and the elephant will be working seamlessly. You will be well on your way to your New Beginning and accomplishing the *what* and *why* you envisioned.

Chapter Reflections

1. It is counterintuitive for fast moving executives and leaders to want to take the time to slow down.... Are you in constant forward motion?

2. To evaluate your Nudges, you need to take the time collaboratively to develop outcome measurements, interim measurements, and drive required activities upfront.

3. Tracking, reporting, and evaluating progress along the way will help you overcome obstacles more quickly.

4. Celebrating successes shows appreciation for a job well done and inspires others to achieve the same type of superior performance. *Roger Bannister.*

5. Applying the TATN communication framework can accelerate your important initiatives. We shared several Customer Stories to show that this works and to give you some ideas.

6. Practice and Reinforce: twenty-one to ninety days and ongoing. This is necessary to achieve your desired results. *Turning Dirt Roads into Superhighways.*

Nudges

1. Ponder these questions: Are you an executive or leader who is always moving to the next initiative (speeding up)? Do you currently take the time to evaluate and celebrate success (slowing down to speed up)? What would your people say?

2. Identify one of your top three Nudges for the year. Do you have outcome measurements, interim indicators, and required activities that can be identified, tracked, and reported? If you do not, please go back and work on these. Then, adapt your Nudge.

3. Identify an accomplished milestone. Go praise the people in your organization who accomplished it. Celebrating success will inspire others to repeat those actions. See how this works and ask yourself what would happen if you repeated this behavior?

A Final Note

Christine and I started this journey with the hypothesis that people and organizations have almost unlimited potential to grow and achieve. Companies want to increase revenue, profit, customer satisfaction, and employee engagement, all leading to increased shareholder value. Individuals want to grow and achieve for their personal satisfaction. However, in order to continue to grow and achieve more, it is imperative to change, and change can be hard and uncomfortable, both personally and organizationally. The old paradigms we have been taught of Nature vs. Nurture and "We are who we are and cannot change" have been big impediments in this endeavor. Christine and I also observed that the world seems to be moving faster; we never seem to have enough time, priorities shift quickly, and we are constantly bombarded with new inputs in our new digital world. Was this change of pace in the world helping or hurting us, as we tried to realize our full potential? Could there be another way to look at this challenge and develop a new solution? We discovered a better way and told you the story of what we learned and how to do it.

By studying the latest research on neuroscience and behavioral economics, we uncovered that there have been some startling discoveries about the power of our brains since 1995 with the use of fMRI technology. This revolutionary knowledge of the brain proved to us that we do have almost unlimited ability to grow and achieve. These studies provided more detailed knowledge of how this marvelous 2.5 pound organism works, causing us to learn new things, rethink some old, and brainstorm. Learning about these profound new developments was key to our understanding, believing, and taking action, as we think it is for you. Along the way, we had an epiphany about Nature *and* Nurture, about "slowing down to speed up," and about using small "Nudges" to get big results. These are some very counterintuitive approaches for our fast-paced world that just plain work.

We synthesized what we had learned about the brain's potential into three key pictures: "The Iceberg," "The Elephant and the Rider," and "Superhighways and Dirt Roads." We thought these illustrations would tell the story of what we learned effectively. We used the pictures to describe more easily the breakthroughs in learning about neuroscience and our brains, especially the idea of neuroplasticity and the ability constantly to build new networks, learning, and do new things.

By applying this knowledge in real-world situations with our clients, we came up with a Communication

Framework, The Art of the Nudge™ (TATN). This is our vehicle or car that we know will help you think about and take action for better results, by harnessing your brain in a new, but easy and comfortable way. Using this approach will help you inspire yourself and your organization to reach greater potential; something we imagine everyone reading this book wants to do.

We introduced and explained three tools that will help you do this: Personality Profiles are the tires of our vehicle and help us to better understand our basic nature, personality, and how we process information; Story is the engine and critical to helping us understand our history, who we are and Why, and our detailed motivations. We developed this framework by utilizing the power of Gathering Stories, and we declare that if you learn to do Gathering well, you can truly create magic in relationships. You can develop and give inspiring stories that will transform and Nudge people to decisive action. The final tool is developing Nudges, which can act as the gas pedal, causing acceleration. We think if you know exactly what you want and *why*—a Nudge—and then develop specific outcomes, interim measurements, and drive required activities, it will guide you on your journey, allowing you to evaluate, celebrate, and adapt. Lastly, we gave you some real customer examples showing specific results, and we recommended a way to practice them consciously to form these superhighways, allowing you eventually to execute in the *flow*.

We are excited to have shared this knowledge with you because we know that by applying it, it will help leaders and organizations that are constantly searching for ways to improve and innovate. We know that the communication framework and tools we have introduced will deliver amazing results and CI^2 is happy to prove it to you.

Lastly, we want to thank you for reading our story, and we hope that our humanness and vulnerability has come through loud and clear. We most certainly appreciate any feedback, ideas, or advice as we, too, continue our journey of learning, growing, and achieving.

John and Christine

ABOUT THE AUTHORS

John Geraci is the Co-Founder and President of CI Squared, a Leadership Development and Sales Training Company. He is a West Point graduate and served six years in the U.S. Army. He had a career in the computer software industry and two breaks in the training business with BlessingWhite and The Complex Sale. He has been working with high-tech  companies over the last ten years, sharing the knowledge he has from his successes and failures and helping people unlock their potential. Along the way, he has continued to learn from these smart customers, while getting extreme satisfaction from his biggest *why*: Helping others grow and achieve. He lives in Reading, Pennsylvania, with his wife Lucia, enjoying his five grown children and three grandchildren, and anticipating the twin grandchildren on the way. His vocations are working-out, playing golf, reading, playing the guitar, and creating memories with his family. *http://cisquared.net/ john-geraci/*

Christine Miles is the Co-Founder and Chief Architect of CI Squared, a Leadership Development and Sales Training Company. She received her M.S. Ed. in Psychological Services from the University of Pennsylvania. Christine is driven by a curiosity to understand what makes people tick and a desire to help others achieve  maximum potential. She has devoted her career to helping people find ways to leverage their talents by developing and improving their emotional intelligence. Early in her career, she was a system's therapist and advocate for families and children; following that, she spent fourteen years working with people and organizations in the Employee Assistance Field. Christine parlayed her earlier experiences into owning her own executive coaching consulting business as a trusted advisor to Fortune 500 companies before forming CI Squared. Regardless with whom she has worked, Christine has seen that increasing one's emotional intelligence leads to greater success, both personally and professionally, and is a key differentiator in talent and leadership development. Witnessing others grow and harness untapped potential has been incredibly rewarding throughout her twenty-nine-year career. Christine lives in North Coventry, Pennsylvania and enjoys golf, swimming, and being a proud aunt to her four nieces (Kristen, Lindsey, Elizabeth, and Ashley). *http://cisquared.net/christine-miles/*

ABOUT OUR CLIENTS

Germantown Academy

Founded in 1759, Germantown Academy is a non-sectarian, coeducational college preparatory school educating students from Pre-K to Grade 12. GA has more than 250 years of history, tradition, and outstanding academics, in which students have been encouraged to follow their passions. The cumulative result is an exceptional academic, artistic, athletic, and social experience that creates successful, well-educated, ethical young people who believe they can make a difference in the world.

http://www.germantownacademy.net/

Compliance Science

Compliance Science is a New York City based global leader in providing web-based regulatory compliance technology and services to the financial services community. In today's complex global market, high-stakes business ventures need help to stay perpetually in compliance with regulatory law and to avoid being vulnerable to financial penalties as well as potentially staggering blows to public relations. Compliance Science helps do just that.

http://www.complysci.com/

SCRA

SCRA (South Carolina Research Authority) was formed by the state of South Carolina with a one-time funding grant of $500,000 and 1,400 acres of undeveloped land. Since inception, SCRA has been self-sustaining. As an applied research corporation, it has over thirty years of experience delivering technology solutions to federal and corporate clients and growing the Knowledge Economy in South Carolina, receiving both national and international recognition.

http://scra.org/

Tozour Energy Systems

Tozour Energy Systems (TES) is a full-service HVAC and building automation provider based in suburban Philadelphia. As the Trane commercial equipment franchise for Philadelphia and South Jersey, TES offers a multitude of climate solutions for commercial buildings with a commitment to delivering superior operating results. Aligning its business with clients' changing needs, TES stays connected throughout the life of every building to measure and improve system performance and energy management continuously.

http://www.tozourenergy.com/

LOOKING AHEAD...
EXCITING NEW RESEARCH
AND MORE TO COME

As we culminate this book project, developing two training programs based upon these ideas (Leadership and Sales), we have actively begun our next research project.

"Leading Leaders in Times of Change" is the title we have picked to describe this next body of work. Our belief is that leaders have to adapt and grow as they lead higher level leaders in organizations of scale, be it business or the military. Although the "Silver Tsunami" will continue to influence markets and the economy, the Millennial Generation is beginning to make significant impacts. Its members have grown up in our digital society, have slightly different values, and are looking for better work and life balance.

In the next several years, we will be interviewing fifty top level leaders to gather their leadership stories, determining whether there are recurring ideas and themes to share. To date, we have interviewed eight distinguished leaders including: Tim Tyson, Chairman of Aptuit and former President of GlaxoSmith-Kline Manufacturing; General David Petraeus, Chairman of KKR Global Institute, retired four-star General and former Director of the CIA; Terri Winslow, former President of Dendrite Software; and Dave Girard the former President and COO of J. D. Edwards.

We will also be interviewing fifty Millennials to gather their stories, discover their *whys*, and learn their views on leadership and work. Using both qualitative and quantitative research techniques, we will analyze both sets of data in trying to identify themes, while juxtaposing what may be significant differences to develop insights.

We believe that leaders will have to continue to adapt and pivot based upon both the fast pace of change in our world and the new values and contributions of Millennials. We believe that TATN is a meaningful way to help accomplish this adaptation, and we hope this research will augment our Communication Framework with robust data leading to insights. We will share this research along the way with blogs and other messages, and if it proves to be significant, in our next book.

Stay tuned for updates on our LinkedIn Company Page, CI Squared LLC, and on our website, http:// cisquared.net.

BIBLIOGRAPHY

Akerlof, George A., and Robert J. Shiller. *Animal Spirits: How Human Psychology Drives the Economy, and Why It Matters for Global Capitalism*. Princeton: Princeton University Press, 2009. Print.

Ariely, Daniel. *Predictably Irrational: The Hidden Forces That Shape Our Decisions*. New York: HarperCollins Publishers, 2008. Print.

Ariely, Daniel. *The Upside of Irrationality: The Unexpected Benefits of Defying Logic*. New York: HarperCollins Publishers, 2010. Print.

Bannister, Roger. *Twin Tracks: The Autobiography*. London: Robson Press, 2015. Print.

Bosworth, Michael, and Ben Zoldan. *What Great Salespeople Do: The Science of Selling Through Emotional Connection and the Power of Story*. New York: Mc-Graw-Hill Companies, Inc., 2012. Print.

Broadwell, Paula, and Vernon Loeb. *All In: The Education of General David Petraeus*. New York: The Penguin Press, 2012. Print.

Brown, Brené. "The Power of Vulnerability." Online video clip. *TED*. TED Conferences LLC, June 2010. Web. 29 Apr. 2015. <http://www.ted.com/talks/brene_brown_on_vulnerability?language=en>.

Campbell, Joseph. *The Hero's Journey: Joseph Campbell on His Life and Work*. Novato: New World Library. 2003. Print.

Chapman, Gary D. *The 5 Love Languages: The Secret to Love that Lasts*. Chicago: Northfield Publishing, 2015. Print.

Collins, Jim. *How the Mighty Fall: And Why Some Companies Never Give In*. New York: HarperCollins Publishers, 2009. Print.

Covey, Stephen R. *The 7 Habits of Highly Effective People*. New York: Simon & Schuster, Inc., 2004. Print.

Dixon, Matthew, and Brent Adamson. *The Challenger Sale: How to Take Control of the Customer Conversation*. New York: Portfolio/Penguin, 2011. Print.

Davis, Paul K. *100 Decisive Battles: From Ancient Times to the Present*. Santa Barbara: ABC-CLIO, Inc., 1999. Print.

Doidge, Norman. *The Brain That Changes Itself*. London: Penguin Books, 2007. Print.

Eades, Keith M., and Timothy T. Sullivan. *The Collaborative Sale: Solution Selling in a Buyer Driven World*. Hoboken: John Wiley & Sons, Inc., 2014. Print.

Goulston, Mark. *Just Listen*. New York: AMACOM, 2010. Print.

Goleman, Daniel. *Emotional Intelligence: Why It Can Matter More Than IQ.* New York: Bantam Books, 1995. Print.

Goodwin, Doris Kearns. *Team of Rivals: The Political Genius of Abraham Lincoln.* New York: Simon & Schuster, 2005. Print.

Haidt, Jonathan. *The Happiness Hypothesis: Finding Modern Truth in Ancient Wisdom.* New York: Basic Books, 2006. Print.

Harris, Michael. *Insight Selling.* Canada: Sales and Marketing Press, 2014. Print.

Hess, Edward D. *Learn or Die: Using Science to Build a Leading-Edge Learning Organization.* New York: Columbia University Press, 2014. Print.

Kahneman, Daniel. *Thinking, Fast and Slow.* New York: Farrar, Straus and Giroux, 2011. Print.

Kaku, Michio. *The Future of the Mind: The Scientific Quest to Understand, Enhance, and Empower the Mind.* New York: Random House LLC, 2014. Print.

McChrystal, Stanley. *My Share of the Task: A Memoir.* New York: Portfolio/Penguin, 2013. Print.

McKee, Robert. *Story: Substance, Structure, Style, and the Principles of Screenwriting.* New York: Harper-Collins Publishers, Inc., 1997. Print.

Medina, John. *Brain Rules: 12 Principles for Surviving and Thriving at Work, Home, and School.* Seattle: Pear Press, 2008. Print.

Merriam-Webster. "Nudge." Encyclopedia Britannica Company. Web. 29 April 2015. <http://www.merriam-webster.com/dictionary/nudge>.

Mlodinow, Leonard. *Subliminal: How Your Unconscious Mind Rules Your Behavior.* New York: Random House, Inc., 2012. Print.

Mlodinow, Leonard. *The Drunkard's Walk: How Randomness Rules Our Lives.* New York: Random House, Inc., 2008. Print.

Neuhauser, Peg C. *Corporate Legends and Lore: The Power of Storytelling as a Management Tool.* New York: McGraw-Hill Companies, 1993. Print.

Neuhauser, Peg C. *Tribal Warfare in Organizations: Turning Tribal Conflict into Negotiated Peace.* New York: Harper Business, 1990. Print.

Patterson, Kerry, Joseph Grenny, Ron McMillan, and Al Switzler. *Crucial Confrontations: Tools for Resolving Broken Promises, Violated Expectations, and Bad Behavior.* New York: McGraw-Hill Companies, Inc., 2005. Print.

Rice, Daniel E., and John Vigna. *West Point Leadership: Profiles of Courage.* Daniel E. Rice, 2013. Print.

Schwartz, Jeffrey M., and Sharon Begley. *The Mind & The Brain: Neuroplasticity and the Power of Mental Force*. New York: ReganBooks, 2002. Print.

Sedlacek, Tomas. *Economics of Good and Evil: The Quest for Economic Meaning from Gilgamesh to Wall Street*. New York: Oxford University Press, 2011. Print.

Shaara, Jeff. *The Last Full Measure*. New York: The Ballantine Publishing Group, 1998. Print.

Shaara, Michael. *The Killer Angels*. New York: Ballantine Books, 1974. Print.

Siegel, Daniel J. *Mindsight: The New Science of Personal Transformation*. New York: Bantam Books, 2010. Print.

Siegel, Daniel J., and Mary Hartzell. *Parenting from the Inside Out: How a Deeper Self-Understanding Can Help You Raise Children Who Thrive*. New York: Penguin Group, 2003. Print.

Simmons, Annette. *The Story Factor: Inspiration, Influence, and Persuasion Through the Art of Storytelling*. New York: Basic Books, 2006. Print.

Smith, Douglas A. *Happiness: The Art of Living With Peace, Confidence and Joy*. Columbus: White Pine Mountain, 2014. Print.

Smith, Paul. *Lead with a Story: A Guide to Crafting Business Narratives That Captivate, Convince, and Inspire*. New York: AMACOM, 2012. Print.

Sinek, Simon. "How Great Leaders Inspire Action." Online video clip. *TED*. TED Conferences LLC, Sept. 2009. Web. 29 Apr. 2015. <http://www.ted.com/talks/simon_sinek_how_great_leaders_inspire_action?language=en>.

Stone, Douglas, Bruce Patton, and Sheila Heen. *Difficult Conversations: How to Discuss What Matters Most*. New York: Penguin Group, 1999. Print.

Straw, Julie, Mark Scullard, Susie Kukkonen, and Barry Davis. *The Work of Leaders: How Vision, Alignment, and Execution Will Change The Way You Lead*. San Francisco: Wiley, 2013. Print.

Van Doren, Charles. *A History of Knowledge: Past, Present, and Future*. New York: Ballantine Books, 1991. Print.

Whitney, David C. *The American Presidents: Biographies of Chief Executives from Washington Through Clinton*. New York: The Reader's Digest Association, 1993. Print.